THE WAR FOR SOULS
IN THE SAN LUIS VALLEY

A Teacher's Story

BY D. REID ROSS

ISBN: 978-0-692-06849-6

The War for Souls in the San Luis Valley: A Teacher's Story

D. Reid Ross

Editor: Elizabeth A. Green
Design and Layout: Lisa Snider

"Never were there so many passions and powers contending
in any other conflict. Never was a field so large.
Never was the crown of victory so dazzling."
– Reverend Albert Barnes

"…when these people became Protestant, it's the letting in of great light
for them in things temporal, as well as things spiritual."
– Anna Marie Ross

PREFACE AND ACKNOWLEDGMENTS

History has been my lifelong passion. A nation that does not know the history of its families does not know itself. By remembering our past and retelling its stories, we gain a crucial memory of our heritage as individuals and as a nation.

I first became interested in American history when I was a fifth-grader in the 1930s. My teacher let me read the entire four-volume, first edition of Carl Sandburg's *Abraham Lincoln*. I was spellbound.

My father's keen interest in history also stimulated me. I learned from him that some of our ancestors had fought in the French and Indian War, the Revolution, the War of 1812, and the Civil War. Looking back, however, I came to realize that he was something of a romantic. There was always a kernel of truth in his remembrances, but finding the kernel was often difficult.

It began to dawn on me that I needed significant insight into how they adjusted to their new environment and how and why they contributed to their new community. To do this, I needed an in-depth understanding of their religious background, the other forces that pushed them out of the Old World, and the opportunities the New World offered that pulled them to start a new life here. I realized that I would need help uncovering the social, economic, and political forces my ancestors had to face. An understanding of colonial and early American history was vital. I also learned that knowing your ancestors brings colonial history alive.

I collected from all my living relatives the birth, death, and marriage records of most of my ancestors. But all I could do with this information was start building a family tree. That was only the first step toward reaching my goal, which was to learn why they left the Old World for the New, what happened to them after they got here, and how that forged their character.

At this point in my research I became interested in learning which ancestors had led the most interesting and significant lives and knew that in-depth additional historical research would reveal their accomplishments. Telling their stories would help me understand the nation's history.

The ancestor I wanted to start with was my great-aunt, Anna Marie Ross.

It was my good fortune to be living in Madison, Wisconsin, when I retired from my career as an urban planner. The University of Wisconsin there not only had one of the best history departments in the country, but also one of the top American history libraries and faculties. At age sixty-two, I enrolled in a few classes and let it be known that I wanted to be admitted as a candidate for a master's degree.

I also let it be known that I wanted to write my thesis on my great-aunt's career as a Presbyterian missionary school teacher with impoverished Hispanic children, in southern Colorado. By then, I had identified the three faculty members I wanted as my thesis advisors, each of whom agreed. One was a professor of religious history; another specialized in history of the American West; and the third was a colonial historian. They were enormously helpful, particularly with mastering the library's vast manuscript collection and recommending books written by social historians like Reid Mitchell.

Each was aware of the amount of research I had already completed and that I was writing an article for the *Journal of Presbyterian History* titled "The War for Souls in the San Luis Valley," which it had accepted. (The article was published in 1987, shortly after I graduated.)

They also introduced me to the enormous historical collections in the Library of Congress and the National Archives, plus the Colorado, New Mexico, and New York state archives and the Presbyterian Historical Society in Philadelphia. I learned to use numerous city and county libraries where she and her New York family had lived. I found that when reference librarians realize you really need and appreciate their help and that you are a serious and competent researcher, most of them will go out of their way to help.

By that point, my father's two ninety-year-old sisters and my oldest first cousin, twenty years older than I was, decided I was serious about becoming the family historian. They began searching for what they had that would help me. My first cousin, then in his eighties, sent me a handmade leather wallet on which my great-grandfather had carved his name, the year 1824, and his residence, Northumberland, Saratoga County. One of my great-aunts sent me a packet of old family letters, the oldest of which was postmarked 1844. The other great-aunt sent an album of family pictures bound in heavy red velvet with carved brass corners. It began with photos taken post-Civil War, including the only photos of Anna's parents and her three living brothers. I cherish these heirlooms.

Shortly before I completed my thesis and the article on Anna and the War for Souls was published in the *Journal of Presbyterian History*, my wife and I decided to retire in Durango, Colorado, where a liberal arts college is located. I could easily do the rest of my family research there. The college subscribed to the Interlibrary Loan system and the Internet's websites and email were as available there as anywhere. I could also access its history faculty and reference librarians when they weren't busy helping students. It proved to be a very wise choice.

I had already done enough research on the Civil War records of my grandfather and his brothers. All four, true to their Scots Reformed Presbyterianism, fought not only to preserve the Union but also to end slavery. All four kept on reenlisting until they became casualties. One was killed in action after three years of service. Another was blinded, the third deafened, and the fourth—my grandfather—was captured and sent to Andersonville prison, in Georgia. Between them, their three regiments fought in almost all major battles. Two of those regiments had extremely high casualty rates. I visited over a hundred libraries to write a book about the Ross brothers. *Lincoln's Veteran Volunteers Win the War* was published by State University of New York Press in 2009.

In addition to that book, in the twenty-eight years of retired life in Durango, I also have had twenty-three articles published in Civil War, historical, and genealogical journals. At this writing, my research into my father's family dates to the early 1600s in Scotland. The earliest of my mother's family arrived in colonial Virginia in 1619.

Researching events and experiences that occurred decades, even centuries, ago has its challenges. In the story of my great-aunt, Anna Marie Ross, I found very little that she herself had written, including a handful of letters to and from her. Digging into records of the churches and organizations that supported her work as a teacher in the San Luis Valley offered some insights. So did reports and records from the Presbyterian Church Historical Society, census records, local historians, and countless librarians.

As with any such endeavor, I encountered gaps and contradictions. For example, sorting through the tangle of names and places was challenging, none more so than a pair of villages where Anna Marie taught. Today the names and locations are clear. Garcia is in Colorado and Costilla is in New Mexico. But in Anna Marie's time there, the names appear to have been interchangeable. My solution is to refer to the villages as Costilla/Garcia, without stipulating which side of the state line was involved.

My indebtedness to the hundred or more reference librarians in the libraries I personally visited while in retirement is profound and humbling. No common cataloging system exists for manuscript collections as it does for cataloging books. Each library has its own system, making help from each reference librarian vital in my search for relevant letters, memoirs, diaries, and other personal records. I am grateful to every one of those librarians, especially Doris McEachron in Washington County, New York, reference librarians for the Presbyterian Historical Society, and Jim Hanson, head librarian at the University of Wisconsin. To all of my relatives who assisted me with information, documents, and photographs, especially those who helped by reviewing my work, I offer my deepest appreciation. And most of all, I am grateful for the support and encouragement of my late wife Sari and our children Janet Ross, Peter Ross, and Kathy Landazabal, who have enabled me to devote thousands of hours, numerous trips, and endless phone calls to my research. Special thanks to Kathy who provided immense help in tracking down and documenting members of the entire seventeen-generation family tree. Thank you.

INTRODUCTION

Anna Marie Ross was forty-seven years old when she enlisted in a war far from home. What mattered most to her were family, faith, and service.

The eldest of six surviving children, Anna Marie was born on a farm in upstate New York to a seventh-generation colonial family of devoted Scots Reformed Covenanting Presbyterians. Their church provided them with a moral compass that guided every choice. As such, they embraced the idea that people should be prepared to do battle for what they believed in. Religious persecution and wars had driven her ancestors from their homelands, and deeply held convictions compelled their descendants to fight in the French and Indian War, the American Revolution, the War of 1812, and the Civil War—no matter what the cost. Anna's commitment to service was rooted in generations of her family's history.

The church and the church-sponsored school with the Bible and the Catechism as its text books were the hallmarks of their church. As a devout Scots Reformed Presbyterian, Anna Marie's dedication to education was within that framework.

Many people in our ecumenical age cannot envision how divisive religious identities were in the United States more than a hundred and fifty years ago. The contentiousness among Catholics and various Protestant groups at that time both created and divided communities, and influenced every aspect of people's lives.

This rivalry had deep roots going back centuries in Europe, from the time of the Reformation in the early 1500s. Each new group that broke away from Catholicism eroded the power of the Church. Exploration and settlement in the Western Hemisphere intensified those rivalries, pitting Catholic countries against Protestant ones. Indigenous populations were converted, by whatever means possible, in order to cement control of New World territories by Old World countries.

In North America, religious pluralism took hold. The primarily Protestant Northeast became a sanctuary for families like Anna Marie Ross's ancestors. To the south and west, Spain held a firm grip on the land and people of Mexico. By the mid-19th century, American expansion disrupted the balance, culminating in the Mexican-American War. At stake were all of what is now Arizona and New Mexico, as well as parts of present-day California, Nevada, Utah, Colorado, and Wyoming. Defeated, Mexico was forced to cede that territory to the United States. What had been a Catholic stronghold was now opened to American settlement, with ample opportunity for grievances and disputes—religious and otherwise.

Religious groups clashed throughout the American West. Following the

Civil War, southern Colorado became a battleground between two distinct religions and cultures: Spanish-speaking Roman Catholics and white Anglo-Saxon Protestants from the Northeast. Other groups joined the fray, including Mormons, who were equally intent on establishing a foothold in the territory.

At the northern frontier of this vast, recently acquired Mexican territory—the San Luis Valley in southern Colorado and adjacent northern New Mexico—Catholics and Protestants distrusted and condemned one another.

Catholics regarded all Protestants as heretics and a great menace to the faithful. In turn, Presbyterian clergy hurled charges of corruption at Catholic priests, contending they stymied both independent personal thinking and the cause of popular enlightenment. Catholic priests criticized the Presbyterian emphasis on individual interpretations of the Bible and what the Church deemed alterations of doctrine to suit Protestant purposes. Priests especially condemned Hispanics who had converted, calling them deserters.

Ministers were making little headway in this standoff, so the Presbyterians changed their tactics. They decided to recruit devout women from the church to serve as home missionary school teachers. Presbyterians were convinced that Hispanics could be "civilized" through Christian charity and education. By 1880 the mission school and its teacher became the means to achieve this end. As Reverend Sheldon Jackson, an outstanding churchman, himself observed, "They won't come to hear preachers; send us a teacher."

As was characteristic for her family, Anna Marie Ross was the first to step forward and answer the call.

This strategy shifted an immense burden from ministers to the shoulders of teachers. These new front line soldiers were committed to the fight, but poorly equipped and minimally supported. Isolation, loneliness, and physical hardship were only part of it. Teachers encountered disheartening coolness, if not outright hostility. Priests labeled them as "corrupt and wicked heretics." Tiny schoolrooms were the norm—poorly built, furnished, lighted, ventilated, heated, and equipped—and attendance was erratic. Teachers were overworked outside the classroom as well, leaving little time for rest and recreation. Abundant tact, patience, and wisdom were needed to overcome suspicion and win the trust and confidence of parents.

Would they be able to meet the demands in such an isolated, hostile setting? Would they win souls for their church?

When Anna Marie left her Ohio home for her new position as a mission school teacher, she had no idea of the resistance she would face. She knew only that she was fulfilling her Christian duty, and would work tirelessly to meet her responsibilities. Her faith would both guide and sustain her through the many challenges she would face.

TABLE OF CONTENTS

A NOTE ABOUT ILLUSTRATIONS

Despite the help I have received from countless relatives, historians, and librarians through the years, I have never found a photograph of Anna Marie Ross. We are left to imagine her appearance, based on photos of her siblings and parents. Nonetheless, without ever seeing her face or her bearing, we can recognize Anna Marie's character through her story.

Charles Wesley Ross

Margaret Reid Ross

ONE

Before the Wars

Charles Wesley Ross and Margaret Reid married in 1830 and settled along upstate New York's Hudson River, just as generations of their families had done before them. Their ancestors had left Scotland and found what they wanted in the colonies: religious freedom and better lives. The couple shared a deep commitment to their Scots Reformed Covenanting Presbyterian faith, an unyielding adherence to God's law, and a firm belief in the supremacy of the Bible.

The Hudson River valley's lush vegetation was deceptive. In some places, the land was far less fertile than native plant life led settlers to believe, and climate made farming all the more precarious. The Rosses were able to supplement their farm income by felling trees from the dense, virgin forests in the winter and floating cordwood downstream to Albany in the spring. They moved their family three times in search of larger farm acreage, more forested land, and improved fertility for growing potatoes, their main crop. As with the timber, they used the river to transport potatoes to larger markets like Albany.

It was always a hardscrabble existence, but Charles and Margaret were determined to imbue in their children all the values that had guided them. The couple's first child, Anna Marie, was born in the summer of 1831. Over the span of fourteen years, Margaret would give birth to four sons and three daughters. All but one, a girl, grew to adulthood. Surrounded by like-minded relatives and neighbors, the Rosses imparted to each of their children an enduring, faith-based moral compass.

Through their childhood, Anna Marie and her siblings heard growing debate over the moral issue of slavery. A basic tenet of their faith taught them that all God's people were entitled to freedom, no matter what their skin color or economic standing. They had learned that the Bible deemed slavery a sin against God and therefore must be eradicated.

By the mid-1840s, anti-Catholic forces also were at work throughout New York State. As historian Ray Billington wrote, "Societies, lectures, newspapers, magazines, churches, ministers, and a political party had all been enlisted in the 'No Popery' movement that even led to violence and bloodshed." Anna Marie certainly must have heard and read such diatribes.

Whether the Ross family brought with them, from the Old World to the New, the deeply felt Scottish anti-Catholic conviction is unknown. They certainly brought the Scots Reformed Covenanting Church doctrine with them and passed it along to at least the next five generations, the last of which included Anna Marie and her five siblings. Specifically, the No Popery sentiment among Protestants in Washington County was strong. In 1837, ninety-four of its residents, many of them Scots Presbyterians, petitioned Congress to determine whether there was "a plan in operation, powerful and dangerous . . . for the subversion of our civil and religious liberties, to be effected by the emigration of Roman Catholics from Europe." This petition was initiated by the preacher of a Presbyterian congregation in that county. There is no record of Anna Marie ever speaking out against Catholicism. Still, she must have at least accepted the church's anti-Popery stance, since she couldn't have received church support if she had openly taken issue with it.

Thousands of miles away, there was growing unrest of a different sort.

Founded even before Anna Marie's Ross and Reid ancestors had reached North American shores, Mexico was Spain's primary foothold in the New World. Explorers had traversed the region in search of fabled cities of gold, to no avail. Instead they found an indigenous population that at first welcomed them, but later rebelled in response to extensive atrocities. For the Spanish conquerors, there was little distinction between government, commerce, and church. Priests were used to subdue and control indigenous people through conversion and strict enforcement of Church directives in their lives.

At the northern extent of Spanish territory lay the San Luis Valley, which is now part of southern Colorado and northern New Mexico. This broad, oval-shaped mountain prairie the size of Massachusetts lies at altitudes of 7,000 to 8,500 feet above sea level, surrounded by 9,000- to 14,000-foot, snow-capped mountains. The headwaters of the Rio Grande are in the mountains on the western side of the valley, the peaks of which constitute the Continental Divide. As the river flows through the southern portion of the valley, it forms the border between Conejos County on the west and Costilla County on the east, before it enters New Mexico.

The valley's earliest inhabitants arrived nearly 12,000 years ago, and it was first continuously occupied by the Utes. Vast aquifers beneath the dry landscape, along with lakes and the river Spaniards would name Rio Grande—Big River—helped make the area an important seasonal hunting ground. By 1400, numerous other tribes had entered the region, including Apache, Navajo, Tiwa, Tewa, Comanche, Kiowa, Cheyenne, and Arapaho.

To encourage settlement of these outlying lands—and thereby overpower the original inhabitants—Spain granted large tracts of land to wealthy Spanish citizens and families, starting in the late 1700s. In 1821 Mexico won its independence from Spain. The territory that encompassed the San Luis Valley was no longer a part of the Spanish colonial empire. After gaining independence, Mexico continued the practice of issuing vast land grants to promote settlement and thereby assert its authority over remote parts of its territory, extending such largesse to French, American, and British men who married Mexican women, as well as to Mexican citizens. These included the 560,000-acre Tierra Amarilla grant in 1821, the 2.5 million-acre Conejos grant in 1833, and the million-acre Sangre de Cristo grant in 1843. Grant holders were required to live on the land, build homes, and foster settlement with construction of walled towns. In return, settlers would have the right to use water, hunt, fish, graze livestock, and harvest timber on pasture and forest lands that were not allocated to individual colonists. The rights of land ownership under these grants, and the use of it by people who did not own it, would prove to be a thorny issue in the coming years.

A French Canadian fur trapper who became known as Charles (or Carlos) Beaubien, settled in Santa Fe and married a Mexican woman, thereby gaining the right to a land grant. In 1841, land east of the Sangre de Cristo Mountains was granted to him and a partner. Two years later, after deeding away part of that land, he sought another million acres west of the mountain range. However, since he was ineligible to receive a second land grant, he had it deeded to his 13-year-old son Narciso and a business partner, Stephen Luis Lee. The 1843 Sangre de Cristo grant extended from the crest of the Sangre de Cristo range west to the Rio Grande. The grant stipulated that the region would be colonized within two years, but Indian raids and war between Mexico and the United States would delay settlement for nearly a decade. Charles Beaubien inherited the grant after his son and Lee were killed in the 1847 Taos Pueblo Rebellion.

The Ross family home in Washington County, New York.

TWO

War in the West

In upstate New York, Anna Marie and her siblings were embracing the values of hard work and education as they reached their teens and considered their future adult lives. Farming was the Ross family's livelihood, but school received equal emphasis, to the point that four of the children decided to become teachers. Public school education ended with the eighth grade, but the Rosses were willing and able to pay for their children's further education.

Anna Marie was the first in her family to attend the Jonesville Academy and train as a teacher. She would be followed by three of her brothers. By her early twenties, she would leave home to teach at a girls' school in Mississippi. Her oldest brother, Will, would also attend Jonesville Academy and then, in 1859, move west to Illinois where work for teachers was plentiful because of rapid population growth. Dan, too, was preparing for a teaching career, and was being urged by his brother Will to join him in Illinois. Lank, a younger brother, was just starting his training at Jonesville Academy when the course of all their lives was altered.

But before any of the Ross children had taken up careers as teachers, international boundaries were radically altered, increasing American territory at the expense of Mexico.

Through the 1840s, Mexico's northern lands were under increasing pressure from American interests. By 1846, the two countries were at war.

The Mormons had preceded all Protestant denominations in thinking about colonizing, or at least exploring, the San Luis Valley. Brigham Young saw the Mexican War as an opportunity to recruit 500 men for the Mormon Battalion. Their pay could be used to purchase supplies for colonization in the West at the end of the war. As they left Fort Leavenworth to join the US Army, Young instructed these soldiers to take careful note of regions favorable to future Mormon settlement. Some members of the battalion left the group when they reached the Arkansas River, and went to Pueblo, where another contingent had settled for the winter.

In the winter of 1846, the remaining battalion assembled at Santa Fe for a march to San Diego. However, a number of the men became ill and had to return to Santa Fe, then continued to Pueblo. Their arduous journey northward took them through the San Luis Valley. Undoubtedly, this was the first Mormon exposure to the valley. By the time the soldiers reached the Sangre de Cristo Pass on December 17, some were severely frost-bitten and two of their mules had frozen to death. About 275 Mormons spent the rest of that winter in Pueblo. With the war ended, they departed around June 1, 1847, for Salt Lake City.

In 1848, the Treaty of Guadalupe Hidalgo ended the Mexican-American conflict, transferring to the United States a vast region from Texas to the Pacific Ocean and north across the Rocky Mountains and Great Basin. Up to 80,000 Mexicans were living in parts of what would become California, New Mexico, Arizona, and Texas, along with smaller numbers in Nevada, Utah, Wyoming, and Colorado. Now they faced a choice: relocate to lands within Mexico's new boundaries or become American citizens. More than 90 percent opted for US citizenship, but they retained their ties to the only religion allowed in Mexico, Roman Catholicism. The treaty safeguarded the place of the church and its property in the annexed territory.

The San Luis Valley was now part of the Territory of New Mexico and would remain so until 1861 when the northern part of the valley was included in the newly created Colorado Territory. With the American promise of protection from Indian hostilities, Hispanic families from the Taos area under contract to Charles Beaubien founded the village of San Luis in 1851, making it the oldest continuously occupied village in what would become Colorado Territory.

Hispanic villages in the San Luis Valley consisted of adobe-walled, dirt-floored houses joined together and built around plazas reminiscent of sixteenth-century Old World cities, as prescribed by King Philip of Spain. There were no outward-facing doors or windows, except for one or two gated entrances at opposite corners of the plaza. The plaza served as a communal gathering place in the daytime and at night as a stockade for cattle and protection against possible Indian raids. Colonists used large fireplaces located in a corner of each adobe house for cooking and heating. These settlers built small chapels shortly after they established villages. Later, as chapels were enlarged to churches, they became the largest structures in town, located at or in the central plaza, where they served as the focus of both social and religious life. Hispanic families had settled southwest of the San Luis area years earlier, on the bank of Costilla Creek in a place they called Plaza de los Manzanares, but the village was never incorporated. This eventually became the twin villages of Costilla and Garcia.

Settlers in the valley pioneered irrigation systems and other agricultural methods that had been employed in Spain. Their San Luis People's Ditch is the oldest in the state to remain in continuous use.

The early Hispanic settlers in the valley received only infrequent visits by priests from Taos and Santa Fe until the Catholics built an adobe chapel and the Reverend Gabriel Ussel offered the first Mass in Conejos in 1856 at Our Lady of Guadalupe. This was the first Catholic church with a resident pastor in what would become Colorado, established by Bishop Jean Baptiste Lamy. In 1852, Bishop Lamy had invited the Sisters of Loretto to build a small boarding and day school in Santa Fe. In 1859, he also invited the Christian Brothers to build boys' schools in Taos and Mora. Father Vincente S. Montano opened a convent in the area and built a rectory in 1860, all blessed by Bishop Lamy in 1863. Expressing their devotion in accordance with Spanish custom, many women of the Conejos parish contributed jewelry, silver plate, and coins to provide metal from which to cast the first church bell.

Rocky Mountain miners who discovered gold in nearby Pikes Peak entered the San Luis Valley in the winter of 1859 and were so stirred "at the sight of the abject ignorance in these plazas that those who could, opened schools to teach Mexican children to read and write. At first these Pike's Peak miners' mission schools were thronged, but soon the priests denounced them and [led] the Mexicans . . . to array themselves against the strangers and to drive them from the villages."

While thousands of Mexicans found themselves swearing allegiance to another country, the Ross children in New York focused on careers and family.

Anna Marie completed her training and accepted a teaching position at the Port Gibson Mississippi Female College, about thirty miles south of Vicksburg, in 1858. The following year Will Ross found a teaching job in Illinois, where private academies were being replaced by public schools. Will wrote to his younger brothers about the opportunities in Illinois, noting that not only could teachers earn $25-$30 a month plus board, but public schools were making education available to all children, regardless of their families' economic circumstances. Dan was wrapping up his studies at Jonesville Academy as his brother Lank enrolled there in 1860. While Dan stayed with his studies, Lank chose to leave school and follow Will to Illinois. Only Charlotte and the youngest brother, John, remained at home with their parents.

No matter what their jobs or employment opportunities, loyalty to family and faith remained at the core of their lives. The children sent what money they could spare to their parents. But as the United States edged ever closer to armed conflict over issues of state sovereignty and slavery, a calling far beyond family would send the four teachers in very different directions.

THREE

Civil War

In December 1860, South Carolina seceded from the Union, followed soon by six more southern states. Calling themselves the Confederate States, they elected a president and on April 12, 1861, captured a US fort in South Carolina. Six more southern states joined the Confederacy, and the nation was at war.

A week after the attack on Fort Sumter, when President Abraham Lincoln called for 75,000 volunteers to serve for three months in the Union army, Will left his teaching position to enlist. Lincoln's initial expectation that the conflict would be resolved quickly proved incorrect. In November, Will re-enlisted, this time for three years. Melancton (Lank), who stayed behind in Illinois, was the next to enlist, on August 10, also for three years. Dan, who finished his studies in June 1861, spent that summer helping his parents on the farm. After the harvest was in, instead of becoming a teacher, he enlisted for three years. Six months later, he was discharged after his cavalry regiment was disbanded because of a lack of horses. Again, he spent the summer on the farm, and then re-enlisted for another three-year term in August 1862.

Anna Marie resigned from her teaching position in Mississippi, rather than remain in a state that was now part of the Confederacy. After the Scots Reformed Presbyterian Church organized its Board of Missions for Freedmen in 1863, she went to Virginia to teach freed slaves.

Their mother pleaded with Will to seek a hardship discharge and return to work on the farm. Margaret and Charles were in poor health, and they needed their sons' help. Will felt a sense of duty to them, but a greater duty to the country and the fight which all the Rosses viewed as essential to finally ending slavery and preserving the Union.

The year 1864 proved disastrous for the family. In April, Lank was blinded on his way to join Sherman's march on Atlanta. The following month, Will was killed in the Battle of the Wilderness in Virginia. In June, Dan was captured and sent to the squalid Confederate prison, Andersonville. Soon afterward, a hailstorm followed by drought and violent winds destroyed most of the family's crops and vegetable gardens. Charles and Margaret Ross were left with little or no income. Nonetheless, their youngest son John enlisted in September, to join Sherman's army in Atlanta. He was determined to take the place of his brother Dan, who remained a Confederate prisoner. That December, during Sherman's siege of Savannah,

Lank Ross

John Ross

Daniel Ross

Will Ross

a shell exploded near John's head, severely damaging his hearing. In spite of his injury and dysentery, when he was released from the hospital, he returned to the army, serving until the conclusion of the war in 1865. In less than a year of service, he had marched 1,200 miles before he was discharged in Washington, DC.

※

At the same time that Anna Marie gave up her teaching job in Mississippi and returned to New York, a widely traveled Missouri lawyer was appointed governor of the new Territory of Colorado, which had been created by Congress in 1861. William Gilpin had attended West Point, fought in the Seminole and Mexican-American wars, and visited Colorado on an expedition to the Pacific Northwest. The gubernatorial appointment by President Abraham Lincoln offered him an opportunity to return to the region along with throngs of gold-hungry prospectors.

Soon after his arrival at Denver City in May 1861, Gilpin took it upon himself to organize a militia, without federal authorization. The action elicited broad criticism in the territory, but he persevered. The lure of Colorado's gold inspired a group of Confederates to invade the territory of New Mexico with ambitions of going on to take over Colorado and even California. Gilpin's Colorado militia played a key role in defeating them at the Battle of Glorietta Pass. Nevertheless, his misstep of obligating the federal government without permission led the president to remove him from office in April 1862.

Although the 1848 Treaty of Guadalupe Hidalgo promised protection of Mexican landowners' and settlers' rights, the vast land grants became a point of contention since they encompassed far more land than Mexican law generally allowed. Nevertheless, in 1860 Congress confirmed Beaubien's title to the entire one-million-acre Sangre de Cristo grant. Three years later, Beaubien negotiated sale of the entire grant to William Gilpin for $41,000—about four cents per acre—with the stipulation that Gilpin would acknowledge the Mexican farmers' rights to land they had settled, including water, grazing, hunting, and timber rights. To help finance colonization of the grant, Gilpin took on several partners. Touting the valley as the finest stock-raising area in the United States, they divided the tract into northern and southern portions and promoted the area to settlers from the United States and abroad.

FOUR

After the Civil War

After the Civil War ended in 1865, the surviving Ross brothers and Anna Marie made their way back to upstate New York and their parents' severely storm-damaged, 107-acre farm. Crippled with arthritis, Charles Ross had been able to harvest only forty bushels of winter rye. Charlotte was gone, having married and moved to live on her new husband's farm. The surviving Ross brothers also were in poor condition. Will was dead; Lank was blind; John was deaf; and Dan was severely weakened by months of starvation and wretched conditions in a series of Confederate prison camps. Nevertheless, Dan left in August 1865 to teach school in West Virginia.

Within a few years Charles and Margaret Ross lost their farm. The debt had grown too large, and the productivity of the land too poor to keep them going, particularly with their declining health. The parents lived with their youngest son John for a while, then bought a tiny farm where they lived with Anna Marie and Lank. Despite what Anna Marie earned as a teacher at Jonesville Academy and Lank earned selling life insurance, Charles and Margaret Ross lost that small farm as well. Most of the family would move away from New York, leaving only John and Charlotte in the Hudson River Valley.

After two years teaching in West Virginia, Dan left to study medicine in Ohio. Following completion of his studies in 1871, he married and established a medical practice in Kilbourne, Ohio. His parents joined him and his new wife in Ohio, but Charles Ross died the following year. Soon afterward, Anna Marie and Lank joined their mother and brother in Ohio. Lank married the sister of Dan's wife in 1875, but by then Dan, his family, and their mother had moved from Ohio back to West Virginia.

Anna Marie remained in Ohio until 1878, likely teaching in some capacity. Then she heard the call for teachers in far-off Colorado.

In his efforts to promote land sales and stimulate development on his southern Colorado land grant, ex-Governor Gilpin appealed unsuccessfully, as early as 1866, to the Jesuit Father Pierre de Smet for help in obtaining schools as well as churches on his land where 6,000 Catholics lived. Gilpin undoubtedly thought schools would help attract colonists, but the Jesuits

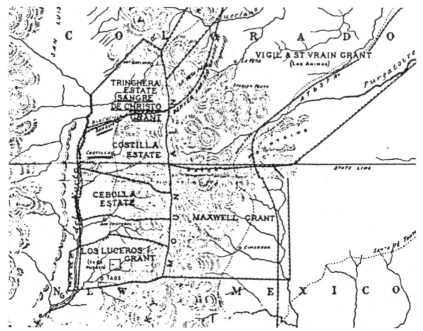

William Blackmore's land interests in Colorado and New Mexico.

were concerned over the plans he and his partner, William Blackmore, were pursuing to attract American and European colonists and preempt the land claims of the Hispanics.

Gilpin sold his interest in the land, in 1872, for an enormous return on his investment, ostensibly the only person to turn a profit on the Sangre de Cristo land grant. He had paid $41,000 for one million acres in 1864 and sold it to William Blackmore for $2.5 million eight years later. It is doubtful, however, that Gilpin ever collected more than a small portion of that amount. Over a span of thirty years, Blackmore, a wealthy Englishman, and his business partners—Dutch bankers, the railroads, the irrigation canal company, and the Travelers Insurance Company—tried unsuccessfully to stimulate land sales. He managed to protect his own interests by personally securing title to 7,500 acres on which his relatives were able to make a comfortable living through sheep ranching and farming. Blackmore sold some of his stock after returning to England, but the rest of the stockholders recovered nothing on their investments. In ill health and suffering severe financial setbacks, Blackmore committed suicide in 1878, at his home in England.

The Denver & Rio Grande Railroad, with which Blackmore had been associated, also exerted its influence in the San Luis Valley. Upon completion in 1875 of its narrow gauge tracks from Denver to Pueblo, the D&RG president, ex-Civil War General William Jackson Palmer, offered a free excursion to the Presbyterian General Assembly. Seventy-five Presbyterian leaders took the journey from Cleveland and in a resolution of thanks stated that "the manifold attractions of this newly opened Territory [have] been verified by our own observation." Had the Presbyterians traveled south of Pueblo and actually entered the valley, their impressions might have been considerably different.

In 1875, army Lt. George M. Wheeler led a geological expedition through the valley, traveling south from Pueblo on a mule, accompanied by a *Harper's Magazine* reporter. The journalist wrote:

> We rode southward over still drearier plains, and through squalid Mexican villages with mud huts and swarthy inhabitants. While we remained on the road we occasionally met a dusty traveler, a burly stock raiser or a light-hearted miner perched on an overloaded donkey, starting out to prospect for gold in the mountains. The wind was bleak and constant, and bore clouds of abominable dust . . . On the tenth day of our travels we reached the town of Conejos, and thence explored a country of miraculous and inexpressible grandeur . . . The canon of the Conejos, the Los Pinos, and the Rio Chama have all the elements of a grand primeval solitude.

The extension of the Denver & Rio Grande from Pueblo to Fort Garland and later into the San Luis Valley, beginning in 1876, introduced a wage economy and a means of transporting sheep to eastern markets. To encourage settlement on the Trinchera Estate, the northern part of the Sangre de Cristo grant, the railroad acquired a right-of-way through it. Railroad construction also brought a sudden influx of Anglo-Americans and the valley became, for a period, a land speculators' paradise. The railroad company attempted to attract, among others, land and livestock enterprises. The "Santa Fe ring" of lawyers and bankers was also involved in legal disputes over land grant claims, railroad deals, irrigation canal construction, and land speculation activity there. In 1878, the railroad founded the town of Alamosa, which became a sizable Hispanic settlement and two years later expanded a sheep herding camp into the small town of Antonito. The speculative boom was short-lived, however, as depression, grasshopper plagues, squatters, controversies, and lawsuits created severe problems.

Nothing is known with certainty about Anna Marie Ross's activities during the years she was in Ohio. However, she had been a dedicated teacher for many years by then, so it is reasonable to assume that she was teaching in some capacity during that time. Whatever her endeavors, they would not be enough to keep her in Ohio, once she learned of a pressing need in the West. Like her brothers' answers to a call for soldiers in the Civil War, she was about to volunteer for a battle that would demand every bit as much deep conviction and sacrifice from her.

FIVE

A New Kind of War

Following the Treaty of Guadalupe Hidalgo, competition for Hispanic souls escalated in Colorado's San Luis Valley, an outgrowth of deep-seated fears among American Protestants. Ministers were eager to dilute the influence of the Catholic Church in the newly acquired territory, encouraged by their churches' governing bodies and congregants.

Concerns about the Catholic Church's influence and control resonated with the Ross family, whose ancestors had fled religious discrimination and poverty in Scotland. In her teenage years, Anna Marie Ross was well-acquainted with anti-Catholic forces, which were at work throughout her home state of New York.

In the early years after the Mexican-American War, efforts focused on converting adult Hispanics who had now sworn their allegiance to the United States. In the years that followed, thwarted Protestants modified their approach by first focusing on children as a point of access to adults and schools as a means of educating people to their view of gospel.

Formed in the mid-1840s, the American Protestant Society had as one of its major objectives the "salvation of Romanists" through protest and missionary activity. Controversy in 1842 and 1843 over whether Bibles—often the only book people had—should be read in the public schools swayed local elections in communities such as Salem, in Washington County, where Anna Marie was growing up. To make matters worse, the Mexican War of 1846-48 pitted the United States against a Catholic power. Even its successful outcome, historian Ray Billington noted, "failed to quiet nativists' fears, for they professed to see in the acquisition of a Catholic-populated domain, only a new plot to surround the United States toward eventual papal subjugation." The religious press helped keep this fear alive.

By the 1860s American leaders in the East were firing up their political artillery, intending to help destroy the foundations of Catholic parochial schools. Former President Ulysses S. Grant assailed church-controlled schools. Nor did Anna Marie and her family escape such strong opinions when they moved to Ohio. A few years before their arrival, Republican Rutherford B. Hayes, as candidate for governor of Ohio, had declared that Democrats were subservient to Rome. James A. Garfield blamed foreign-born radicals for the railroad violence of 1877. While Boston and New York elected their first Irish Catholic mayors, reflecting the growth of the Irish population, the Presbyterian Reverend Samuel D. Burchard preached

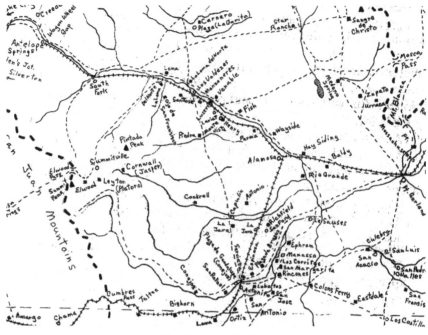

The San Luis Valley

against "Rum, Romanism and Rebellion." The anti-Catholic Order of the American Union was organized with its membership open to all Protestants, regardless of birth. And the charismatic Rev. Sheldon Jackson, superintendent of Presbyterian Home Missions for the Rocky Mountains Region, became an honorary member of the national Anti-Papal League.

Jackson's sentiments were echoed by Reverend George Darley, who opened the Presbyterian College of the Southwest in 1884. Presbyterians were, he asserted, "at the very front of the Christian Army." But Darley went further, adding "filthy Mormonism" to his list of foes.

The Catholic Church's tight hold on the hearts and souls of the region's residents was about to be challenged on numerous fronts, including the San Luis Valley. Methodists, Lutherans, Baptists, and Episcopalians all sought to establish churches in the Southwest, principally, however, to serve Anglos, not Hispanics. The Anglo-American settlers who pioneered Colorado and New Mexico had matured in an era of anti-Catholic sentiment, if not hysteria. Many Protestants feared Catholics were plotting to dominate the West. One early Presbyterian arrival wrote, "it is high time that Christians were waking up out of their sleep . . . The enemy [is] straining every nerve."

Reverend Albert Barnes most eloquently expressed the religious fervor in this War for Souls from the Protestant perspective. He was a leading Presbyterian publicist and advocate of the Home Mission effort and had been a leader of its New School abolitionists. To these religionists he wrote, "The West may now be regarded the great battle-field of the world . . . far reaching and mighty. [This will] determine what shall be the governing mind of this vast land. Shall it be [barbarism], infidelity, Roman Catholicism, or evangelical religion? Never were there so many passions and powers contending in any other conflict. Never was a field so large. Never was the crown of victory so dazzling."

Methodists had arrived in the valley as early as 1866, when the Reverend John L. Dyer, the circuit-riding "Snow Shoe Itinerant" and presiding elder of the Colorado Conference, preached in Ft. Garland to the soldiers garrisoned there. The fort was located in the middle of this vast north-south valley. From there, he preached to about thirty Hispanics who gathered at the ranch of a Mr. Tobin, whose wife was a Mexican Catholic. Dyer returned somewhat later to learn that Father Joseph P. Machebeuf had convinced Tobin that the missionary should not be allowed to preach there again. He was told that "none but Catholic clergy could solemnize marriage or do anything right."

Dyer was also convinced that sermons given in English lost their "fire" when translated by Spanish-speaking interpreters. He was certain that a better-educated man was needed "to take hold of the Spanish work and elevate those who were starving for the gospel." He realized that Protestant missionary work would not be easy. Privation, hardship, loneliness, fatigue, illness, and even physical danger had to be faced. Bitter opposition was guaranteed from Catholic priests who would not tolerate any disturbance of the religious status quo of "The Church."

Dyer could not speak Spanish. With 78 percent of the population over age ten illiterate, a preaching ministry would have to be accompanied by a teaching ministry in the Spanish language. Nevertheless, in 1869 and 1870, he preached two more times in private homes in Saguache County.

It was not until ten years after Dyer's arrival, that Methodist churches were established at the north end of the valley, one in Del Norte in 1877 and the other in Saguache, thirty-five miles apart. One preacher served both congregations, which together totaled twenty-nine members. Susan B. Anthony gave the dedication speech for the Del Norte church. Neither church had a school attached to it.

In 1888, (fourteen years after his arrival in Colorado,) Episcopal missionary Bishop John F. Spaulding ("the Bishop of all Outdoors") rode a stagecoach for 140 miles though the northern end of the "enchanted San Luis

Valley." In Monte Vista he established a mission church in a stone replica of a small English church.

Initially, three forms of Catholicism were practiced in the valley. One form was espoused by Father Antonio Jose Martinez. Father Martinez was a very popular and liberal priest who taught that the Bible was the word of God and advocated freedom of religion. French-born Bishop Jean Baptiste Lamy, a Franciscan who arrived from Kentucky with the first papal appointment as Vicar Apostolic of New Mexico at Santa Fe and whose supervisory duties included the valley, excommunicated him in 1858 for his liberal views.

A second form of Catholicism was Penitential. The Penitentes were Hispanic laymen who followed a brand of popular folk Catholicism reminiscent of the medieval Spanish Roman Catholic penitential tradition, which was transplanted to the New World by the conquistadors. The Penitentes embarrassed the clergy, particularly because of their Good Friday ritual when they publicly whipped a cross-bearer in the ceremony and supposedly crucified him. In fact, a troop from Fort Garland stormed into the San Pedro Plaza during the early 1860s to prevent the "murder of the cross bearer."

The third was led by native priests trained in the province of Durango in old Mexico at the time the spirit of Mexican independence was peaking. These Hispanic priests resented American occupation. Bishop Lamy largely disavowed them. He regarded the "Mexicans" as both intellectually and morally unfit to be priests.

In 1868, the Roman Catholics established the Vicariate Apostolic of Denver and placed the Catholic missions in the San Luis Valley under another French-born bishop, Joseph P. Machebeuf. Before the Presbyterians arrived, the Conejos parish had become part of the Denver mission. At one time the parish included some twenty villages and *placitas,* including San Luis and San Pedro where the Church erected small chapels in 1859. Prior to this, visiting secular priests from Taos under Santa Fe's Vicar Apostolic had infrequently served small chapels built in 1852 in San Pedro and in 1856 in San Acacio for Hispanics who were not Penitentes.

When the first permanent Jesuit missionaries arrived in the San Luis Valley in 1871, only a few years before the Presbyterians did, they assumed responsibility from the Franciscans. The Jesuits were convinced that Almighty God had a great purpose for them—to help the clergy defend and maintain Catholicism and to oppose Protestant fanaticism and bigotry. These sins would spread rapidly, facilitated by the railroad network, already under construction. Accordingly, the Catholics adopted a military-like plan.

The Jesuits established the Conejos mission with a resident Neopolitan Jesuit priest, Father Salvatore Persone. Two additional expatriate brothers from Naples, Italy, joined him during the next year and "there began a religious revival the like of which had never before been seen in the San Luis Valley." These priests found about 3,000 inhabitants in the twenty-five villages that they visited in the valley during 1872. Their revivals were held to strengthen the parish against anticipated Protestant encroachment. The parish diary kept during the Lenten season of 1872 reads as follows:

> Considering the lamentable state in which the people lived, the Fathers sought a means of urging and getting them to fulfill their religious obligations. The time was very favorable, for it was the Lenten Season, and much more so because it was winter, when the people live shut up in their huts, while in the summer they are so scattered that it is impossible to gather them together. Hence, the two Fathers began to visit the villages and the ranches, going from house to house, and confessing almost everyone in his own home. To be sure, almost the whole night went in hearing confessions, there were boys and girls and also adults who had not yet made their First Communion. But God lightened this work with almost 2,000 confessions, with eight persons who left the bad life, with the removal of other less public scandals, and the destruction of many Protestant books. . . . The fact is that since the Fathers arrived the people come to Mass, go to confession, [Penitentes'] abuses and scandals are being removed, and the people live in peace and without fear of being attacked and killed.

By 1872, the Jesuits in northern New Mexico were concerned about the rise of anti-Catholic forces they attributed to the construction of the Atchison, Topeka & Santa Fe Railway, which by 1881 would reach Las Cruces and the Southern Pacific. To offset these forces, they brought a printing press to Santa Fe to print books of instruction and piety; started a series of missions, revivals, and a college; and by 1875 were also printing a weekly newspaper, *La Revista Católica*, to defend the faith against Protestant missionaries and the railroads. Its first editor was one of the Neapolitan Jesuits recruited in 1872 to conduct the revival in the valley. The newspaper was circulated in the San Luis Valley as well as in northern New Mexico. This military-like plan was designed to be both offensive and defensive in protecting the Catholic faith from perceived attacks by Protestant "fanatics and bigots." As one historian noted, the Jesuit order was "militant by nature and born of conflict … it jealously manned the religious bastions of the Mother Church, defending Pope and Faith against the Protestant assault and the railroads."

By 1877, the Presbyterian newspaper *El Anciano* began publication by the Reverend Alexander Darley to counter charges by *La Revista Católica*, A lively newspaper debate over the relative merits of each group's schools and religious dogma ensued. Details of this face-off in the press can only be gleaned from rebuttals in the columns of *La Revista Católica* since the only copy of *El Anciano* known to survive is the first issue. Still another, *La Aurora*, was published by Gabino Rendon. Each obviously perceived the other paper to be riddled with errors that needed to be unmasked.

By 1878, the church authorities had redrawn the Conejos parish boundary to coincide with the Conejos county limits, and the Church of San Miguel in Costilla/Garcia became the parish seat for Costilla County. Both parishes were under the Vicariate Apostolic of Colorado. Thus, Conejos and Costilla/Garcia became the two command posts from which the Catholics directed the battle in the valley, with Jesuit priests in charge at Conejos and secular priests at Costilla/Garcia. By 1891, the parish seat of Costilla County had shifted again to the Church of the Precious Blood in San Luis and Father R. Garassu became the regular resident pastor.

Some thirty years after the first Mormons had attempted to settle the area, Elder John Morgan, a Mormon missionary in Georgia and Alabama and an ex-Civil War officer in Sherman's Army, reported to Brigham Young that some of his converts wanted to settle in the Rocky Mountains. Young agreed to this in the hope that the converts could also do missionary work among the Indians and Hispanics. Furthermore, overpopulation had become the major economic problem Mormons were facing in Utah's Great Basin. To solve it, at least 100 new Mormon settlements were established outside Utah between 1876 and 1879.

Desiring employment for his colonists so that they could earn funds to buy farm land and equipment, Morgan contacted A. C. Hunt, former territorial governor of Colorado, who was a promoter for the Denver & Rio Grande Railroad. Hunt wanted settlers at the southern end of the valley where the next extension of the railroad would terminate at Antonito. Visiting the area, Morgan found the soil suitable and satisfied himself that the railroad would be extended that far and jobs would be available. The Mormon Church loaned the original colonists sufficient money to buy two small ranches which, in some cases, had been occupied by Hispanic "squatters" who had built adobe houses on them. About fifty Mormon colonists began arriving in late spring 1878, after being recruited by Morgan in Georgia, Alabama, Mississippi, and Virginia. Other colonists came from Utah and New Mexico, bringing the total to about 150, who settled in the village they named Manassa by the spring of 1879. Jack Dempsey and his sister were born here. He later became known as the "Manassa Mauler," while she became the town prostitute. The Latter-Day Saints believed that "Conejos County will be the most likely place to start opening up the gospel to the Mexican people."

Mormon Bishop Hans Jensen, who was experienced in town development and irrigation canal construction, arrived from Utah to initiate these two activities, together with James Z. Stewart, a bilingual missionary. A log church was among the first buildings completed, and/ the colonists rented an existing twenty-by-forty-foot house to use as a school, as well as for church services and public meetings. John Allen was the first teacher. Mormons began efforts to proselytize their Hispanic neighbors almost immediately, alarming the Jesuits in Conejos.

Virtually on his own, Presbyterian Reverend Alex Darley initiated a whirlwind evangelizing campaign starting about 1875 to convert the Penitentes and other Hispanics to Presbyterianism by distributing the Bible and building churches. He believed that the virtually unarmed Presbyterians "were opposed by the mighty opposition of the Roman Papacy." Colporteur Albert Jacobs of the American Bible Society assisted him by distributing Bibles door to door at this time. Darley encouraged the Presbytery of Colorado to support his work as the railroads that were being built into the valley would attract new farming and ranching activity. He argued that the Hispanics were ready to adopt Anglo-American political ideas, social customs, and institutions. He organized the Presbyterian Hispanic congregation at La Jara in 1878 on that assumption, while Presbyterians established eight more congregations during the 1880s and four in the 1890s.

The editor of the Jesuit newspaper *La Revista Católica* attacked Darley for his efforts to evangelize in La Jara, asserting that devout Catholics collected "Bibles, books, and brochures" that Darley distributed "by the handful" and threw them "onto the bonfire." Collectively they signed a letter to the editor of the newspaper proclaiming, "We are Roman Catholics, and Spanish by blood, and . . . the blood will sooner be sucked from our veins, or our hearts snatched from our chests than [allow] the Catholic faith [to be] wrested from our souls."

The Presbyterians sought converts wherever they could find them, even by holding services for the miners in saloons. "I do not give any notice of these services," wrote one missionary, "but just go quietly in with a policeman and ask the permission of the proprietor to sing, pray and preach, and then, permission being given, mount the platform and commence." The Colorado Presbyterians supported temperance and opposed dancing, divorce, prize fighting, and horse racing. Darley reported converting a noted prostitute in 1877, in Del Norte, Colorado.

Clearly, the Mormons, Catholics, and Presbyterians utilized very different organizational approaches to winning the souls of the Hispanics. The Mormon approach was to colonize because Utah was becoming "too crowded" for them. They used their own church members to build Mormon villages with their own schools for their own children. They also built irrigation ditches and virtually everything else necessary to create the most successful agriculture-based society and to help relieve the overpopulation problem in the Great Basin of Utah. By being the most successful economically, however, they also set an example for farmers that was hard to ignore. Nevertheless, the Mormon villages were apparently too close to the Jesuit stronghold in Conejos to proselytize successfully. As the Jesuits noted in 1885, "God did not permit his flock to fall into the jaws of these ravenous wolves, and the attempt . . . failed from the beginning."

The Catholic approach was to use priests—Jesuit and secular—to spread the word on a person-to-person basis. The Bible and other printed tracts were not employed to convert a largely illiterate population. The churches they built were almost always the largest buildings in the villages, located on the plaza and used as the center of religious as well as social life for the community. As a result, every villager had frequent contact with the Catholic Church, one way or another.

Shortly after the Colorado Territory was established in 1861, legal provisions were adopted for establishment of public schools. Parents of school age children could initiate the action by petitions, specifying proposed school district boundaries. If two-thirds of all parents voted in favor, a school board would be elected and a school tax rate would be set. However, no such action took place in the San Luis Valley. Lacking any government funding, the only "public" schools in the valley were fee-based.

Traditionally, schools had been virtually nonexistent among the Hispanic Catholics. They were considered a luxury of the elite, wealthy families who could hire teachers for their own children or for a small group of families taught in their own homes. Although the Jesuit Fathers of the New Orleans Province established a mission in Conejos in 1871, it was not until 1875 that the Hispanic settlers in Conejos asked the Jesuits for a school. Each *placita* to be served agreed to assume responsibility for the cost of building one or two schoolrooms. In response, with the approval of Bishop Machebeuf, in 1877 the Jesuits brought the Sisters of Loretto to Conejos from Denver. Three nuns—one Hispanic and two Irish—opened a convent. With the assistance of Maj. Lafayette Head, they also opened a coeducational parochial school known as Guadalupe Academy, thus establishing the beginning of an educational Jesuit community. It was the only Catholic school in Conejos County. Instead of establishing their own schools, the Catholics otherwise trained teachers to serve in public schools.

At the outset, the Presbyterians—particularly Alex Darley—were evangelical in their approach. Like countless missionaries before him, he had a well-established hierarchy of tasks: preach the Gospel, circulate the Bible and other tracts, build a church, and then establish schools.

The Presbyterians were not discouraged in their missionary work by widespread opposition from the Hispanic population in the San Luis Valley. The Reverend George Darley, Alex's brother, who had initiated Presbyterian efforts there in 1875, viewed his potential converts through a lens of cultural bias, "Wherever I went, I found them to be as lazy mortals as ever lived," but this characteristic did not excuse mistreatment or discourage mission work by the Presbyterians.

Presbyterians recognized that they could not reach the adult Hispanic population in direct competition with priests who had a two-century head start in establishing trust and rapport. Presbyterians regarded Hispanics, like Native Americans, as "exceptional populations" to be reached only through their children. They based their final approach, therefore, on the assumption that illiterate parents wanted and needed something better for their children. To improve their lot in an Anglo-dominated society, Hispanic children required an education. The Bible and the Catechism became textbooks in the Presbyterian mission school classroom, but they were not the only textbooks, and the public school teachers did not use them at all.

Protestants accused Jesuits of wanting to break up the common school system of the area and using public funds to finance denominational schools, especially their own. They also charged that Catholics had to pay priests for baptisms, marriages, and burials and that from the age of fifteen until death parishioners were obligated to maintain the church and all its property, regardless of how poverty-stricken they might be. In 1879, *La Revista Cathólica* answered these and other denunciations with vigor.

Following the Civil War, Presbyterian women claimed an increasing role in promulgating their faith. They began to define their area of church service as that of educating the "exceptional populations" of western America:

"Indians, Hispanics, and Mormons" who needed extra proselytizing to convert them to Presbyterianism. They dedicated themselves to woman's work for women and children, i.e., supporting female missionaries, teachers, and Bible readers, and educating students in missionary schools. They did this initially through the Woman's Board of Home Missions, supplementing the efforts of the various boards of the Presbyterian Church.

Other Presbyterian women's organizations also were dedicating themselves to education. The Santa Fe Missionary Association, founded in Auburn, New York, recognized the value of schools on the frontier, establishing its first one in Santa Fe in 1867. The New Mexico, Arizona, and Colorado Missionary Association, also organized in New York a year later, paid teacher salaries, purchased schools, and distributed reading materials. Still others were the Women's Union Missionary Society, whose purpose was "to furnish the ignorant Romanists of New Mexico [and Southern Colorado] with religious teachers, and raise funds for their support"; and the New York Ladies Board of Missions. They were all convinced that exceptional populations could be reached only through their children. These organizations were not only creating means to reach children; they were opening a new profession for women.

By the early 1870s the Reverend Sheldon Jackson and the Reverend Henry Kendall, secretary of the Board of Home Missions, clearly realized the need for schools as much as churches among non-English-speaking, illiterate people. Jackson learned that with both Native Americans and Hispanics, "it was absolutely necessary to establish mission schools to prepare the way for the preaching of the gospel."

In sharp contrast, Alex Darley, an ardent evangelist, clung to the nativistic American Bible Society belief that converts could most efficiently be won by distributing the Holy Book combined with the American Tract Society's use of colporteurs to distribute these and other religious tracts, and to plead with Papists to change their faith. As late as August 1880, Darley wrote, "As far as work in Colorado is concerned, I am impressed with the wisdom and necessity of a church organization before a school organization. The order of work best to be followed being: The Bible and colporteurs, the preacher and the church, the teacher and the scholar."

The first and only issue of the Spanish language paper, *Revista Evangelica*, was published in July 1877, a year before woman teachers would join the War for Souls in the valley. Reverend John M. Annin, its editor, stated the publication's purpose was to provide support "for education, morality and true religion of the native people," the Hispanics. The means by which he proposed to reach his goals was establishing schools for the young, on the premise that there was no greater need for the good of the Hispano population than to provide the "schoolhouse, the primer, the school teacher, and some stimulus to the mind."

Colorado Territory had been established in 1861. Fifteen years later, it became a state, the thirty-eighth in the Union, with its capital on the other side of the mountains in Denver. The following year saw the first public school districts and public schools established and teachers employed in the San Luis Valley. However, compulsory education in southern Colorado was not mandated until 1899. The first public high school for Spanish-speaking residents was not built in either Costilla or Conejos counties until after the turn of the century.

By 1875, the New York Ladies' Board of Missions called for presbyteries throughout the state to organize women's missionary societies independent of the Woman's Board of Home Missions. The result was a proliferation of locally organized women's missionary groups. Delegates from churches in Syracuse and the surrounding communities of Baldwinsville, Jamesville, Skaneateles, and Fayetteville, where a number of Anna Marie Ross's extended family on her mother's side lived, organized the Women's Presbyterial Missionary Society of the Syracuse, New York, Presbytery in April 1877. The purpose was to "diffuse intelligence, to excite missionary interest among the people." Members of Anna Marie's family belonged to several of the churches in this Synod. In 1878, the Colorado Woman's Synodical Society also was organized at the urging of Sheldon Jackson.

By 1877, action by the Presbyterian Colorado General Assembly finally laid the groundwork for the Board of Home Missions to build schools before churches to serve the exceptional populations, and to use women teachers and Bible readers. This decision was based on the realization that after eight years of concerted efforts in the San Luis Valley, educating children while hoping they eventually would respond to the Gospel was more effective than traditional preaching by a Church-oriented ministry. The Reverend Sheldon Jackson (a native of New York State) and the Reverend Henry Kendall, secretary of the Board of Home Missions, were promoting a separate entity: a woman's organization to undertake the activity. By the end of 1878, the Women's Executive Committee of Home Missions was created exclusively for this purpose.

From their beginning in 1878, Presbyterians would eventually establish thirty schools for Hispanics in New Mexico and southern Colorado. That achievement stemmed largely from Jackson and Kendall's efforts to organize the Woman's Executive Committee of Home Missions on the national level and Presbyterial societies on the local level among Presbyterian women.

Although Anna Marie Ross was residing in Ohio at this time, she maintained strong ties with relatives and friends in Syracuse and other towns in Onondaga County, New York, where most of her extended family still lived. What was happening there surely played a part in her response to the call for teachers in the San Luis Valley. At the first annual meeting of the Syracuse Women's Missionary Society in April 1878, its president read a letter from Henry Kendall addressed to all Presbyterian women. It appealed to them for aid and offered to commit to them "the whole educational work of the home board in establishing and maintaining schools." The Syracuse women responded by organizing a number of committees to visit every church in the presbytery where there was no ladies society and seek to establish one. A number of Anna Marie's relatives—aunts, uncles, and cousins—who belonged to some of these churches undoubtedly informed her of this action. She, in turn, must have told them of her intense desire to serve. The Syracuse Society would continue to pay her salary until at least 1890.

Immediately following this activity, the Reverend Nelson Millard, Pastor of the First Church of Syracuse, attended the May 7-8, 1878, meeting of the Colorado Presbytery in Denver. The Reverend Sheldon Jackson also was present at this meeting as was the Reverend Alex Darley, who successfully introduced a resolution that bilingual missionaries "could establish schools and preach with great success to both American and Mexican people" at Walsenberg, Trinidad, Conejos, and Costilla/Garcia. This resolution called for three men to assist Alex Darley toward that goal and also called for the formation of a Ladies Home and Foreign Missionary Society to assist the Colorado Presbytery in opening churches and schools in these villages. Darley and others believed that Hispanics in Colorado "were more free from papal servitude than those in New Mexico."

Others besides Jackson and Kendall would differ with Alex Darley over the issue of which should come first in the valley: churches or schools? evangelizing or teaching? In 1877, both the Reverend James M. Roberts, of the Santa Fe Presbytery, who recommended hiring Anna Marie Ross for her first teaching job in the valley, and the Reverend John Annin, who participated in founding the school in Mesilla, New Mexico, where Anna Marie also would teach, made their position abundantly clear that the schoolhouse was the most imperative need. Reverend Roberts had organized the first Presbyterian church in the valley, at Cenicero, in 1876, the year before he recommended hiring Anna Marie Ross. It was received into the Santa Fe Presbytery. He also recommended hiring five teachers at annual salaries of $500. By 1882, in *Presbyterian Home Missions*, the Reverend John G. Reid would characterize the mission school as the vital opening wedge to the ultimate establishment of a church.

The Presbyterians therefore took their War for Souls among people of all classes. They were eager to do battle with the Catholics, employing as their basic strategy the location of schools where support from local community leaders gave them a foothold and where they could keep their costs as low as possible. To conquer the religious frontier, their invading force was to be teachers. As the Reverend George Darley, brother of Alexander Darley and president of the Presbyterian College of the Southwest in Del Norte (opened in 1884 with a faculty of three from Ohio to serve both the San Luis and San Juan valleys), told his audience on a fund-raising trip to New York Presbyterian churches in 1884:

> Geographically we are at the very front of the Christian Army. The war-whoop of the savage has but just now ceased among our hills. On the west we are face to face with filthy Mormonism, on the south with hoary Romanism, and both [are] inexorable enemies. But these grand mountains, and these vast valleys, with all their immense capabilities, are the Lord's. In his name and by his strength we intend to take possession, and today is the day to begin.

SIX

— · —

Soldiers in the War for Souls

I f, as historian Katherine Bennett noted, the years 1870-1880 consti-
tuted the "Church Woman's Decade," Anna Marie Ross was in the right
place at the right time. The Presbyterian women who committed themselves to providing the leadership, funds, and supplies for home missions
through national and regional church organizations needed other women as
troopers to "work for women and children." One such organization, a front-
runner in this movement, was the Women's Presbyterian Missionary Society
of Syracuse. In April 1877 it proposed to "infuse intelligence, to excite missionary interest among the people."

In 1878 Anna Marie Ross was forty- seven. A tall, stern, and angular
woman, she had been a teacher and principal before the Civil War in a small
female college in Mississippi and after the war in a coeducational finishing
school near her New York home until it closed in 1871. Like her four brothers, she would now become a soldier. But she would be a different kind of
combatant—an educator. In a letter to Sheldon Jackson, Henry Kendall described her as "a self-reliant and experienced teacher." She was, by all ac-
counts, deeply serious, thoughtful, and studious.

Eager for the experience and for the greatest challenge of her career, Anna
Marie had written to Sheldon Jackson as early as August 1877. Most likely
while living near Columbus, Ohio, she first met Jackson in 1875 when he
spoke to a joint meeting of four synods—Erie, Western Pennsylvania,
Cleveland, and Columbus—to propose the formation of a Woman's Board
of Home Missions. Her brother Dan, by then a doctor, had moved to West
Virginia the year before, along with his wife and their mother. Their father
had died shortly after moving to Ohio. Their brother Lank, who had been
blinded in the Civil War, was married. With her immediate family taken
care of, Anna Marie was free to pursue her ideals.

Jackson forwarded her letter to the Reverend James M. Roberts in Taos,
New Mexico. After reviewing her credentials, Roberts replied to Jackson, "I
will open a correspondence with her at once." Meanwhile, she received the
endorsement of her church in Kilbourne, Ohio. Roberts had arrived in the
San Luis Valley in September 1877 from Taos to organize the first Mexican
church at Cenicero (near Antonito) and the second in Costilla/Garcia in
1878. Previously, Roberts had served as a missionary to the Navajo Indians
and had helped to found the Presbytery of Santa Fe in 1868.

As a result of this flurry of effort in Colorado, Ohio, and New York,
Anna Marie obtained her commission as a missionary teacher during the

summer of 1878. In the September 1878 issue of *The Rocky Mountain Presbyterian* (which became the official organ of the Board of Home Missions), Roberts issued a call for eight teachers. This call was made with the understanding that:

> they are not to be sent out except as individuals, after churches, or ladies societies [agree to] pledge their support . . . the ladies are ready to go and the Board [of Home Missions] to send them, but the funds are wanting. Who will pledge $500? Who $300? . . . there is need of haste.

Before going to Colorado, Anna Marie returned to her home state of New York, where she visited a number of ladies' auxiliaries of the Syracuse area churches so "that they might become acquainted with her, and interested in her work, and also in her support" and to receive the endorsement of the Syracuse Presbytery. The Syracuse Women's Missionary Society pledged $500 to pay her first year's salary. Their early support would enable her to answer the call and become one of the first two missionary school teachers to serve in the San Luis Valley. The group continued to raise money for her salary as well as for other teachers for a number of years thereafter. But with only a financial shoestring to keep the effort alive, she would have to maintain profound dedication to fulfill the pledge.

Anna Marie Ross and Susie Pitts, of Knoxville, Iowa, were the first to reach the valley in response to the call. Although the Board of Home Missions was crippled by debt, on the recommendation of Reverend Roberts, it commissioned them to serve and agreed to pay a salary of $500 to Pitts. With the Syracuse group's contributions, the Board initially would not have to pay anything toward Anna Marie's salary. The women arrived in October 1878, having traveled by "iron horse" as far as Alamosa on the Denver & Rio Grande Railroad, which had been opened to that point on the Fourth of July, just three months previously. Known as the "Baby Railway of America," it was initially the longest narrow gauge railroad in the world. For the last forty miles, the two teachers traveled by stagecoach or wagon to San Luis, an all-Catholic community of about 100 families, in Costilla County. There Anna Marie was to open her first school in the valley. Pitts was to open a school in Costilla/Garcia. Traveling charges per day at that time were seventy-five cents each for a horse, a meal, and a bed. There is no record of who paid the women's travel costs.

By 1878, Catholic Church authorities had redrawn the Conejos parish boundary to coincide with the Conejos county limits, and the Church of

San Miguel in Costilla/Garcia became the parish seat for Costilla County. Both parishes were under the Vicariate Apostolic of Colorado. Thus, the villages of Conejos and Costilla became the two command posts from which the Catholics directed the battle in the valley, with Jesuit priests in charge at Conejos and secular priests at Costilla/Garcia. By 1891, the parish seat of Costilla County had shifted again to the Church of the Precious Blood in San Luis and Father R. Garassu became the regular resident pastor.

Placement in an all-Catholic community presented Anna Marie with a challenge greater than any of her fellow teachers because the village did not support a Presbyterian church. All other schools in the valley were associated with a Presbyterian church, which provided some financial and other assistance to them.

Anna Marie arrived without any preparation whatsoever for dealing with the poverty or the cultural and religious traditions of the all-Catholic Hispanic population, much less the intolerable winter weather. It is inconceivable that she could have envisioned the overwhelming hardships of the life she was about to enter. As Edith Agnew and Ruth Barber, long-experienced Presbyterian educators and administrators, wrote in their book *Sowers Went Forth*, early Hispanic settlers in the valley "eked out a barren existence from the arid soil, [confronted by] Indian depredations, [and] political intrigue from Spanish and Mexican rulers [and indifferent] neglect from the U.S. Congress."

It is doubtful that she brought with her any knowledge of the Spanish language, although she undoubtedly soon developed a partial command of it. Her recorded teaching experience had been limited to the female academy in Mississippi, where daughters of middle- and upper-class Protestant families attended, and the coeducational academy in New York where she and her brothers studied. She had also tutored freedmen in Virginia, and likely taught public school in Ohio. Her social and personal lives were circumscribed by her close-knit, Covenanting Scots Presbyterian extended family and village, to all of whom she felt intense loyalty. She was particularly loyal to her younger brother, who would be a West Virginia doctor for fifty years, and in whose home she would spend the last eleven years of her life.

In October, immediately after her arrival, Anna Marie requested Spanish Bibles, which the American Bible Society donated through the Syracuse Women's Presbytery. The Syracuse women sent them to her "together with bed quilts and a number of useful articles." The responsibilities that the Syracuse Women's Missionary Society assumed under the model charter for a local woman's committee were within the guidelines of the Woman's Executive Committee for Home Missions. Over the years, these guidelines directed local committees to "support Missionary teachers, to furnish facilities for their work, to prepare 'boxes' for families of Home Missionaries and teachers, to send clothing when needed for pupils in the schools, to aid in building and furnishing Chapels and School Rooms."

Within a few weeks after Anna Marie's arrival in October 1878, Reverend Roberts, her first supervisor, sent an initial report about her back to New York headquarters. In the report addressed to Henry Kendall, Roberts described an elder in one of his churches who was "prejudiced against lady teachers." Roberts had convinced the elder to visit the new school at San Luis. "He was not a little surprised and greatly pleased with the performance of our excellent teacher there[,] Miss Ross[,] and is not only willing but much pleased to do all he can to support a lady among his own people at Ceniseros [sic]."

Meanwhile, the Colorado Presbytery raised $950 by its October 1878 meeting to implement the decision it had made at its May meeting to open churches and schools in southern Colorado. After hearing this report, the Reverend Sheldon Jackson introduced a resolution, which was adopted, urging all preachers in the Colorado Presbytery to organize Women's Home Mission Societies in their churches. The prospective school at Conejos was also "endorsed to the public for $500." By 1880, the Colorado Presbytery agreed also to pay salaries of $500 to teachers at Cenicero, La Jara, San Rafael/Mogote, and San Luis, all of which were in the valley.

The Syracuse Women's Missionary Society continued to pay Anna Marie's $500 annual salary until at least 1890 and to send her boxes of school supplies and clothing until 1893. Over the years she wrote letters to keep them posted as to what she was doing and occasionally made personal summertime visits to update them and undoubtedly encourage financial support. At least nineteen churches within the Syracuse Presbytery contributed between $2.50 and $60 annually to her support. The Reverend Henry Kendall also addressed them on several occasions on the work of the Board of Home Missions. Likewise, the Colorado and later the Pueblo Presbytery met the expenses of Anna Marie's school as well as that of others and paid the salaries of several teachers.

Anna Marie's first winter in the valley was severe. The *Denver Daily Tribune* reported on November 15, 1878—six weeks after her arrival—that the lower half of the San Luis Valley had experienced a snowstorm that lasted nine days, the worst in the memory of the oldest inhabitant. On the coldest night of the storm, the temperature dropped to minus 44 degrees. The snow was accompanied by a fog lasting two days, so dense that stagecoach drivers lost their way, some for twenty-four hours.

In December 1878, Anna Marie moved out of the home in which Roberts placed her, started a boarding house, and took on one boarder for companionship. Roberts reported to Sheldon Jackson that: "Miss Ross is a good teacher. She is waiting untill [sic] the arrival of the Evangelist [likely Alex Darley] to begin a Sabbath School," the first to be organized for Hispanic children. With the additional self-imposed workload of running a boarding house and a Sunday school, she had to believe that "idle hands are the devil's workshop."

As a result of overwork, combined with the severe climate to which she had not yet adjusted, she became ill and remained so through part of the winter. Pitts had to assist her. During her illness or shortly thereafter, she wrote the Board of Home Missions, offering to give up a portion of her salary if a friend from Delaware, Ohio, were hired to assist her. She noted that under these circumstances "the salary of another teacher with mine would be only $100 more than mine now is." Mrs. Julia Graham, president of the Home Missions Board, however, wrote Sheldon Jackson that the Board "could not incur [this] enormous expenditure for so few scholars."

Within two months after Anna Marie arrived, on December 13, 1878, the Costilla County superintendent of schools wrote the state superintendent of public instruction a most heart-rending plea on behalf of the Mexican families in the county:

> Now, I should think, the State would do something to assist the so-called degraded Mexican population, who notwithstanding have their offsprings and are as fond of them as white parents are, and [who] strain every nerve to support their children, and many they have, such knowledge as can be procured by the scanty means of county taxes. . . . The latter a burden hardly to be met . . . by the impoverished, half starved people, who for the last five years had to see . . . their meagre crops . . . devoured by the greedy grasshopper during one night [dashing] the fond hopes of many a Pater familias, who can not keep the wolf from the door. The winter has set in with unusual severity.
>
> The parents of the little ones have one consolation, they know their children visit the public schools, learn something and are enabled to warm their shivering bodies the greater part of the day in the schoolroom.
>
> Please dear Supt. let me know, what you can do for the poor children of Costilla County. . . . You will be blessed, your name

gratefully mentioned in every hut and hovel.

This eloquent plea netted the county $218.04 in state school funds, arriving in time for use during the next school year. Clearly, Anna Marie and Pitts and the other teachers yet to come had their work cut out for them and no one knew it better than the county superintendent of schools. Roberts and Jackson, however, had known for some time that most of the teachers they were recruiting were equal to the task.

The Presbytery of Santa Fe also adopted a salary schedule for teachers, including $500 annually for Anna Marie Ross. At least some of the money for those salaries came from groups like the Syracuse Women's Missionary Society, which continued to raise money throughout Anna Marie's tenure in the San Luis Valley.

Pitts, whom Henry Kendall described to Sheldon Jackson as "young and inexperienced," opened her school at Costilla/Garcia, a village of almost 300 straddling the New Mexico/Colorado state line. Roberts became a circuit-riding preacher, ministering to congregations at Cenicero, Los Sauces, San Rafael, and probably La Jara and Costilla/Garcia as well. He reported in an undated letter written in early 1879, "Miss Ross has 15 pupils and is doing well. If Miss Pitts does not become discouraged she will soon overcome all obstacles, have a reasonably good school and do very well." Both had been instructed to open and close school each day with a prayer. However, they were authorized to excuse children from praying if their parents objected.

Later in 1879, in response to her rapidly growing workload, Anna Marie received a volunteer unpaid assistant. Lizzie B. Smith was the daughter of a professor of Greek at Jefferson College in Philadelphia. Anna Marie wanted companionship badly and believed strongly that teachers should work in pairs.

Other than the Guadalupe school in Conejos, the Presbyterian mission schools were the first to be established in Conejos and Costilla counties. By 1890 there would be sixteen schools with an enrollment of 1,933, two-thirds of the school-age population.

In 1879, Jesuits noted that if the Mormons who were based in Manassa succeeded, "everything, and religion above all, would have been deeply threatened, especially since among the Catholics, many were of very weak faith." By 1882 a second Mormon settlement, Ephraim, was established near Manassa and a school built there. The two towns organized a public school district, operated three Sabbath schools, and had a combined population of about 600. Manassa became the seat of the San Luis Valley stake, and several wards were established by 1883. By 1886 it was estimated that the Mormon population of the San Luis Valley had increased to 1,000 and the Hispanics to 10,000.

As would prove to be the case with the Presbyterians, the Jesuits had little to fear in losing the War for Souls to Mormons.

The Reverend Alex Darley opened the third Presbyterian school in the valley in 1879, at La Jara, after he organized the third Mexican church in the valley. Malana Conaway, who wrote and spoke Spanish fluently, became its first teacher and had forty students enrolled in three months. Like Pitts, she was from Iowa, but since 1874 had lived in Colorado, where she probably learned Spanish.

Apparently, this assignment was made after Roberts wrote Jackson in early 1879 asking that he not send Darley among the Conejos people. He added if Darley "is a preacher he must open a school at once. [However,] I do not think [he] is the man to teach." In August, the Presbytery of Santa Fe recommended that its stated clerk write the Board of Home Missions urging it to instruct Darley to abstain from all ministerial duties in Cenicero. In fact, Darley's old-style evangelism, together with his personality as supervisor, proved nearly disastrous to the morale of all the troops. Fortunately, Jackson rectified the problem in short order. Both he and Henry Kendall had known of Darley's shortcomings for some time. In December 1879, Kendall wrote Jackson, "No one doubts Darley's energy—but I think every man that knows him doubts his prudence . . . and as to putting him in control of Miss Ross and all the school work—never, never."

In 1879, Reverend Alexander Darley asked the American Bible Society for a Bible colporteur in the valley. He also described in the *Rocky Mountain Presbyterian* a 444-mile horseback trip he took through Costilla County when he visited the new school teacher at Costilla/Garcia [Susie Pitts]:

> [She] says she will teach whether the Home Board can commission or not . . . [and] we were [also] able to give the Lord's supper to our faithful teachers at San Luis [Anna Marie Ross and Lizzie Smith], long deprived of gospel ordinances, and who, in their hunger therefore had driven forty miles, to Alamosa, for preaching two weeks before, to hear their first sermon in months, because we have no resident preacher in Costilla County.

Meanwhile, Ferd Meyer, a merchant in Costilla/Garcia, offered Susie Pitts a house in which to teach his children "and take such others as will come." She wrote the Board of Home Missions that this would relieve them of her salary and that, while it might cut off some of the Hispanic children from her school, it would enable her to teach the Bible freely, and conduct a Sunday school and other Christian exercises. By March 1879, these arrangements were complete. Pitts was now employed by the merchant.

According to a letter Kendall wrote to Jackson in 1880, Anna Marie was thinking about teaching in a public school as well. Referring to such moves into public schools, Kendall wrote, "All right. The more of that, the better. It gives us good teachers and Christian women doing good work at the expense of the state."

Sheldon Jackson and Henry Kendall were guided by the belief that schools were needed as much as churches, that illiterate and non-English-speaking populations had to be reached through their children. Jackson further believed that educating children would also have a double appeal to the women in Home Mission Societies because they could employ women as teachers.

To partially solve the problem of teachers being isolated, the church authorities created the Presbytery of Pueblo in 1880 to serve southern Colorado, and Darley became its head. By 1880 Anna Marie also was teaching a Sunday School class of eighteen in San Luis where the 1880 census records her as the only school teacher living in the village. A public school also was in existence, operating for four to five months during the winter, beginning in December but for boys only.

Jackson was in Colorado Springs in May 1880 to attend the meeting called by the Colorado Synod to found the Pueblo Presbytery. He also visited the San Luis Valley at Kendall's request to resolve the problems created by Reverend Alex Darley with the Hispanic church elders, Roberts, Anna Marie Ross, and other school teachers. Kendall wrote Jackson in May, "Miss Ross you must see. She is not certain she ought to continue at San Luis." Jackson himself probably told the presbytery at the May meeting that the Board of Home Missions lacked "confidence in the wisdom of Brother Darley's management."

Leaving Darley's ego, trigger-temper, and impulsiveness aside, the bone of contention was over which should come first—the church or the school. Darley was the only one to argue that churches should precede schools in the valley. Further, he had a very patronizing attitude, referring repeatedly to "my Mexicans" in correspondence. The Hispanic elders at the church, particularly in Cenicero, resented his paternalism and did not want to deal with Darley. Yet they trusted Roberts and wanted a school with a teacher like Anna Marie Ross.

Meanwhile, the Board of Home Missions was making its first ecumenical attempt, in cooperation with Methodists and Baptists, to establish a church,

The plaza at La Mesilla, with its church and famous twin bells, trader waggons on the Santa Fe–Chihuahua Trail, and a woodsman with his burro-load of wood. From an anonymous painting of the period, c. 1860s

Sabbath school, and missionary school in a small southern New Mexico town, Mesilla. Each denomination was too small to function on its own. They recruited the Reverend Thomas Thompson, M.D., to be the preacher and needed a teacher to direct the school.

Anna Marie wrote to Reverend Jackson from San Luis on June 14, 1880:

> As I am more and more convinced that I ought to make a change of climate before another winter, I very gladly accept the appointment to Mesilla. . . . If I am sent there without Miss Smith I want a good teacher of both vocal and instrumental music as my associate teacher. . . . You know music would about double our receipts besides greatly helping to put us beyond the reach of the 'Powers that be.' . . . If Miss Pitts [of Costilla/Garcia] were free she would like to teach with me.

Her dissatisfaction with Darley as her supervisor and his evangelistic approach also had motivated her to seek the transfer to Mesilla, about 400 miles south of the San Luis Valley, near Las Cruces. In her letter, Anna Marie also asked if she could take her bedding with her or just her clothing.

She took a month's vacation to recuperate and mull things over. This may be the only vacation she took in her fifteen years in the valley, other than several summers when she returned to New York to raise money for teacher salaries and school supplies, and subsequently to visit her brother in West Virginia.

Lizzie Smith would not be joining Anna Marie in Mesilla. She had transferred from Anna Marie's school to La Jara earlier that year. When Darley opened the fourth mission school in the fall at San Rafael/Mogote, Smith became its first teacher. He established a church in conjunction with the school shortly thereafter.

Mesilla, with a population of about 2,000, was founded in 1850 by sixty families of colonists. In 1870, a Methodist missionary had reported that not a single public school existed in the entire Territory of New Mexico, describing it as "one of the darkest corners of Christendom." However, by August 1872, The Reverend F. O. Barstow, an Episcopalian, had opened a school shortly after his arrival at Mesilla. It was known as the Grace Church Mission. The Reverend John F. Spaulding preached there to stimulate interest in an Episcopal church, which opened its doors in 1875. Barstow's adobe house, in the meantime, served as an academy and a chapel. He wrote, "Nowhere on this continent are good schools needed more than in New Mexico." Apparently this school was operated to serve children of Anglo families and "the better class of Mexicans," who presumably spoke English. This school lasted only a year or two. Another, however, was established in 1877 by the Episcopal Diocese of the Rio Grande and was known as the St. James Mission School. Its principal and sole teacher was George R. Bowman. According to the *Mesilla News,* when the school's second term began in 1878, children were "received on easy [financial] terms."

In November 1878, the newspaper *Mesilla Valley Independent,* reported that "the only public school which had been open for only eight months was suspended for want of means. There is no school building but on solicitation one could be erected." In December it noted that "the great number of boys and girls in our streets is prima facie evidents [*sic*] of the need for a public school."

Sheldon Jackson's effort to establish a Protestant foothold in Mesilla was designed to counter the work of the five Catholic Sisters of Mercy whom Bishop John Baptiste Salpointe dispatched in 1880 to Mesilla from Ireland, and via Santa Fe, to open a school. Two of these sisters took the public school examination and obtained their certificates but did not teach until several years later.

By late summer Jackson arrived in Mesilla and attacked the Sisters of

Loretto because a novice of their convent was supposedly seen at midnight outside the convent as a Jesuit priest arrived in his buggy. Shortly afterwards, they scandalized the community by eloping. Protestants apparently used this incident to convince parents to "take their daughters out of the convent of the Sisters and put them in a mixed and non-sectarian school." In so doing, they would no longer be exposed to the moral laxity of nuns and priests and would be free from the orders of the "old gentleman in Rome."

By early September Anna Marie left the San Luis Valley for Mesilla, where she opened the ecumenical mission school. She was replaced in San Luis by Susie D. Grimstead sometime after November. Upon her arrival in Mesilla, she again wrote to Jackson on September 9, saying, "Here I am safe and sound, cot, bedstead, etc. Only I left my large trunk at Socorro to be sent down on a freight wagon."

On September 13, 1880, Anna Marie opened her schoolroom with some students that were "anxious to have school begin." Her arrival in Mesilla coincided with clashes between the Sisters of Loretto and the Sisters of Mercy. "The Lincoln County War" also erupted, initiated by the infamous Santa Fe Ring. It led to violence by "hired guns," lawlessness, bloodshed, murder, brawls, land grabbing, sheep and cattle rustling, posses, illegal liquor sales to Indians, and Indian raids. Mesilla's peak of notoriety occurred in April 1881, when "Billy the Kid" was tried for murder of the Lincoln County Sheriff and found guilty on May 13. He was sentenced to "hang by the neck until his body be dead," but escaped.

Once again, Anna Marie Ross—undoubtedly chosen by Jackson—was in the front lines of the confrontation with the Catholics. In October 1880, Reverend Thompson reported to Jackson from Mesilla that "our school has started well—we have twenty-one students—five of them are Mexicans. Kendall was not satisfied. In November, he wrote Jackson, "I have seen Miss Ross's note to you about a 2nd teacher and yet she has five Mexican children out of a total of 21! Some of the American scholars want to study the higher branches—we are not giving High School advantages to American children! We sent her to the Mexican children and if she can't get more than a dozen or half that [number]—ought we to continue the school?"

Part of the exasperation Kendall expressed in this correspondence may be due to a growing concern that his soldiers might not be enthusiastically fighting the War for Hispanic Souls that the church was waging. Pitts was already teaching Anglo-American as well as Hispanic children through arrangements made by Ferd Meyer. Now Anna Marie was teaching a preponderance of Anglo-American children. Perhaps the thought crossed

Kendall's mind that she was merely fighting a war against illiteracy because she regarded education of children as an end in itself, whether they were Hispanic or Anglo-American. Others were concerned that these children would also "come under Romish influence, were it not for the school." Nevertheless, Anna Marie had to be given credit for the fact that the school she started opened its doors before both the Sisters of Mercy school and Reverend Thompson's church, which had only ten members.

At a meeting of the Board of Home Missions Sheldon Jackson is known to have reported on the work of Miss Ross—her methods of teaching, subjects taught, characteristics and attendance of the pupils, and the problems and prospects of her school. Unfortunately, the contents of that report cannot be found.

Not only did Kendall and Jackson agree with Anna Marie that education should be the first priority of a missionary effort, but some Presbyterians in New Mexico also did. Reverend John Annin, editor of *Revista Evangelica,* stated in the prospectus of the first and only issue of that publication in 1877 that "the school house, the primer, the school teacher and some stimulus to the mind of New Mexico's men and women, boys and girls . . . [is the] most imperative need today."

In early 1881, Jackson and Kendall must have decided to abandon the effort at Mesilla after the school year ended. Anna Marie Ross was transferred back to the front lines in San Luis. This decision may have been based on the small number of Hispanic students enrolled in the school, although there were perhaps other reasons as well: a new presbytery had been established to serve southern Colorado; Alex Darley appeared to be on his way out of the picture; two young and inexperienced teachers had just arrived; Conaway and Smith had been ill for part of the previous year; and at least one older teacher, Susie D. Grimstead, was discouraged and despondent in the valley. They needed a staunch warrior and self-reliant teacher who could set an example, pull things together, and rebuild troop morale until a commander arrived on the field. The minutes of the April 1881 meeting of the Pueblo presbytery record that the teachers in the valley were "subject to much discouragement."

Returning to San Luis was wholly acceptable to Anna Marie, who had been unnerved by the violence erupting almost continuously in Mesilla, plus the murder trial of Billy the Kid. On May 17, 1881, at the end of the school year, she wrote Jackson that "Miss Grimstead [who had successfully 'toughed it out' in Siam doing missionary work] has very little hope that anything can be done in San Luis and indeed the obstacles do seem almost insurmountable." Yet, Anna Marie added, "I feel like making one more effort for my dear people there." She explained, "Wherever I may be located, I hope to be in some measure under your watch and care." Clearly, she was expressing her loyalty to the general in charge of the War for Souls he had initiated and in which she was the first to enlist.

She closed the school in Mesilla in June 1881, writing Jackson that "it is too warm to teach there during the summer weather. . . . The asthmatic trouble for which I went to Mesilla has not returned, and I am able to keep house and teach without feeling much the worse for it." She was succeeded in Mesilla by a Miss KcKean, but shortly thereafter the school was closed and the building put up for sale.

The next teachers to arrive in the valley, in 1881, were two graduates of Park College, Missouri, Jennie E. Kipp and Mary B. Higgins, whose annual salaries of $300 each were met by the Woman's Board of the Southwest. Kipp was from Cameron and Higgins from Osborn, Missouri. Higgins succeeded Smith at San Rafael/Mogote and taught thirty-eight students. There is no record of where Kipp taught, or how long she stayed. Each had an organ donated to her school by the Ladies Missionary Society of Parksville, Missouri.

By September 1881, Anna Marie was back in San Luis teaching. Before her move to Mesilla, the 1880 census of the village had recorded ninety-two households and a total population of 341, including eighty school age-children. Only twenty-two (one-fourth) of these, however, had attended school at some time during the census year. Nine of the ninety-two households were non-Hispanic. Two doors away from her lived Charles H. Brickenstein, a Presbyterian who was listed as "a 20 year old clerk, s.o." [sales clerk?], but who eight years later was the Conejos County school superintendent, undoubtedly encouraged by Anna Marie to fill this position. In 1888, he established seven new school districts and opened two schools in the county. The year before that, only two schools existed in all of Conejos County: San Rafael/Mogote and Guadalupe Academy. In 1889 he became county treasurer and served for ten years in that capacity, and among other duties collected the taxes that supported these schools.

Non-Hispanics in San Luis village were relatively few in 1880. Among them were some neighbors, including Joseph Snodgrass, a carpenter, and his wife (James C. Snodgrass was postmaster 1884-1887); Joseph Guttler, a carpenter born in Prussia, and his Hispanic wife; Mary Blackmore (wife of George Blackmore, brother of William, the land speculator), her mother and two brothers (they lived next door to Anna Marie); Dr. Joseph Kugler, born in Württemberg, Germany, and his Hispanic wife, who lived next door to the Blackmores (Dr. Kugler served as Costilla County superintendent of schools from 1881 to 1883). Also listed were: Louis Cohn, a merchant born in Prussia (who relocated his first store from Costilla/Garcia to San Luis in 1871 or 1872); his next-door neighbor Nat Nathan, also a merchant and Cohn's cattle-raising partner (Nathan was born in New York of Prussian parents); George Easterday, who operated a flour mill, and his wife (Easterday's father Harvey had moved to San Luis from Taos to build and manage the mill); and Alexander St. Glair, a blacksmith, and his Hispanic wife. (St. Glair had responded in 1869 to an ad Easterday placed in a St. Louis newspaper seeking a millwright to help build his mill.) At various times, Dr. Kugler, Louis Cohn, and Harvey Easterday had served as elected officials of the San Luis school district. Almost all of these families also had children, many of whom were Anna Marie's students.

Soon after her return to San Luis, Anna Marie was again at odds with Darley. But the year brought changes in the leadership of Presbyterian Home Missions. Ill health forced the Reverend Roberts, Anna Marie's original supervisor, to leave his post. The Reverend J. J. Gilchrist of the Presbytery of Indianapolis had arrived in June as the new Home Mission supervisor. He delivered his first sermon in Spanish in September, assisted in the translation by Conaway. Shortly thereafter, Gilchrist reported conditions to Jackson in two letters. The first indicated that there was dissatisfaction with Darley at every step. "Evangelists out of humor—one with this and one with that, three teachers [Ross, Grimstead, and Conaway] disgusted with him, and laughing at his wild remarks." Conaway, who was at Cenicero, soon quit to teach in an American school. In Gilchrist's personal view, Darley "had tried to be a general and failed. There was too much boss, and the boss had soured. . ." Even Jacobs, the colporteur, was upset with Darley.

Alex Darley finally left the San Luis Valley in 1882, and was replaced by Reverend W.W. Morton. Like his predecessor, Morton clashed with people and lasted only through the winter.

Despite the dissatisfaction among the teachers, Gilchrist reported a few months later that four schools under his supervision were in operation at the beginning of 1882, with five salaried teachers and one unpaid. Only one of these schools was in Costilla County, San Luis; it was taught by Anna Marie with Elizabeth M. Gilchrist (Rev. Gilchrist's sister) as her assistant, teaching music. The others were in Conejos County at Cenicero with Effie J. Miller as the teacher (its first term was only two months long), San Rafael/Mogote with Mary Higgins and Lizzie Smith, and La Jara with Susie D. Grimstead. Higgins initially taught twenty-six students. By June, Grimstead reported that enrollment had increased from seven to twenty and all attended Sunday School. All schools were full except for the one taught by Anna Marie, whose enrollment suffered a temporary setback. Higgins' enrollment soon increased to thirty-eight students who brought their own seats—a box, a bench, or chair. She wrote that they needed a blackboard, seats, and a school bell. In the three-year period 1878-1881, the Presbyterians had clearly established a beachhead.

In January 1882, Anna Marie reported to Jackson that her school had seventeen pupils. She wrote that four of these were Mormon children from Manassa, adding, "There were nearly thirty in school previous to Christmas but by that time the 'Powers that be' [Mormons] took the alarm and started an opposition school. They have enticed away seven of my little Mexicans. . . . I think no one could ask for a more enthusiastic welcome than the people of this place gave me upon my return from Mesilla. . . . The padres have started an opposition Sabbath school also, that has brought [my] Sabbath school down from 35 to 15." She also reported she had her commission made out for Costilla County rather than just the village of San Luis so that she could do some vacation work elsewhere if the opportunity arose. By May, she relocated to Costilla/Garcia, twenty miles from San Luis, and helped to organize a church with sixteen members, the fifth in the valley. Schools opened and closed at different times, and operated for different lengths of time, so it is possible that Anna Marie continued to work with Gilchrist in San Luis at least some of the time.

After her return to the valley Anna Marie soon realized the Presbyterian churches were not receiving many converts. In a January 26, 1882, letter to Reverend Jackson, from San Luis, she noted Albert Jacobs—a newly appointed colporteur and evangelist—had told her of "quite a Protestant awakening at San Acacio," a few miles west of San Luis. She added that she had "heard nothing of it from any [other] source." She also reported in the same letter that she did know of one Mexican convert "but I know of no other tokens for good in this vicinity." This guarded language suggests she was pointing out that if there were a school in San Acacio there also would be more Hispanic converts. In June, the Syracuse Presbyterian Society reported they had raised $551.89, slightly more than her salary.

On July 18, 1882, Anna Marie reported opening a fifth school in Costilla/Garcia in a letter, which undoubtedly described lives of the five missionary school teachers working with children, their parents, and other adults.

> La Costilla, 7, 18, '82. School opened here (on the Colorado side of the town) the 3rd inst. Have registered nineteen pupils, and

a Mexican was in, this P.M., to say he would send one of his children tomorrow, and if that one does well he will send me five of his children all winter. If that boy does not learn, it will be because he is not capable.

The church will no doubt sound to you as something very small, but to me, after working nearly four years among the Mexican people, and knowing so well how hard it is to reach them, even such a beginning is full of encouragement. One man has come into the church since I came here, making seventeen adults in all.

Our licentiate [Jacobs] seems to be doing a work here. No one knows the Mexican people better than he does, or how to approach them if he will only do what he knows is right. There is plenty of work for me outside of school duties, and it is work that I like to do. When these people come into our church they need teaching just like children who unite with a church, only they lack the child's teachable spirit and comparative innocence. Still, we must do the best we can for the parents, and hope for better results from our labor among their children.

It is very gratifying to have the parents anxious to have their children learn the Catechism in the day-school, so all those whose parents do not object to it are drilled in the Child's Catechism (Spanish of course) twice a day. There are two little boys in school who shut their mouths up very tightly and look down at the floor every time they were called up with the rest for the catechism, so I took the first opportunity to ask their mother (a Romanist) if she and her husband objected to their children learning the Catechism. She said, "yes, they did object, and had intended to ask to have the children excused from it." So those two sit at their desks while the rest recite. It is my private opinion that they will know as much of the Catechism as any other children in the school.

When this letter was written, the Reverend John G. Reid, superintendent of missions for the Colorado Presbytery reported that the work in southern Colorado was so enlarged that the Reverend J. J. Gilchrist had been assigned by the Board of Home Missions to the San Luis Valley. His headquarters were at Alamosa, and in his presbytery there were five churches, the newest one having just opened at Costilla/Garcia, where Anna Marie Ross was teaching nineteen pupils. For several years the school was to have no regular quarters. The other churches were in San Rafael, Cenicero, Agua Caliente, and De Herera. Additionally, there were three "licensed elders" or "native helpers" who served as door-to-door evangelists. Among other publications, they distributed *El Anciano*, the Spanish language religious monthly initially published about 1877 by the Reverend Alex Darley at Alamosa and later by Gilchrist. Its anti-Catholic bias was readily discernible.

Reverend Reid explained the importance of schools in the valley and the life of the teachers as he saw it:

> We regard the mission school . . . as an opening wedge, preparatory to and laying foundations for the ultimate establishment of a church, or else serving as an instructive agent alongside of a church . . . so long as the Romanists maintain their almost exclusive control of the politics of these more remote districts, there is little hope of securing free public schools. . . . In the San Luis Valley we at present have four schools. [not including the new school at Costilla/Garcia] The work of the teacher is far from easy. All alone, miles away from any white friend or associate; living by herself in her school room through the long winter months . . . with her school work often discouraging.

The number of schools (five) and churches (five) had increased sufficiently so that in October 1882 the Reverend Henry B. Gage of the Presbytery of Pueblo reported the need for a "minister to take charge of the group of Mexican churches and schools in the San Luis Valley. His work will have to be almost entirely in the Spanish language," Gage wrote, adding, "With only one exception, most encouraging reports come from every field. Churches are becoming strong and are reporting more and more received on profession of faith."

In October 1882, the Pueblo Presbytery dispatched the Reverend T. C. Kirkwood to fill the position of minister in the San Luis Valley. Anna Marie and Kirkwood must have been important influences on each other. Like her, Kirkwood had grown up in Saratoga County, New York, and was a devout Scots Reformed Presbyterian. They were about the same age and both mastered the Spanish language.

SEVEN

— • —

A New Strategy

Five years into Anna Marie Ross's service in the War for Souls, the priorities shifted. The Presbyterian leadership came to realize what she already knew: the bigger battle was against illiteracy, not Catholicism. A combination of circumstances created the opportunity for the Pueblo Presbytery decision to mobilize collectively and to convert the War for Souls into a war against illiteracy, with the teachers as the front line troops. The presbytery was meeting in the valley for the first time, in January 1883, and its members received a first-hand account from the teachers and elders.

Anna Marie had already decided to re-orient her efforts and undoubtedly had the backing of Jackson and Kendall. The reverends Roberts and Reid had advocated this strategy previously. Darley had opposed it but he had been transferred elsewhere. Five schools—San Luis, San Rafael/Mogote, Costilla/Garcia, Cenicero, and La Jara—were now staffed and funded, each operated in conjunction with a church.

Shifting the classroom focus would not put an end to efforts toward converting residents to her faith. It would simply relocate those efforts. Teaching in the schools remained the foundation for a church serving children's parents and other villagers, so as to deliver the spiritual message to all the adult population of the village.

Anna Marie had repeatedly demonstrated her talent for recruiting students and teachers, organizing schools as well as churches, and raising financial support for the work she and other teachers were doing. She had received the toughest assignments and demonstrated her self-reliance and courage. During the four-plus years she was on the front she had built three schools—San Luis, Mesilla, and Costilla/Garcia. She mastered Spanish by reading her Spanish Bible and Catechism at night and recruited a volunteer music teacher. She had learned that Hispanics preferred to read, write, sing, pray, and preach in Spanish. She had organized Sabbath schools in San Luis as well as in Costilla/Garcia a few months previously, and spent most of her summers conducting Bible readings in Spanish in village plazas and once in Alamosa. She called this "vacation teaching."

Other summers, she went back east to raise money. She also taught adults and was already thinking about the need for a girls' boarding school. She had earned the respect of Hispanic elders, the missionary preachers, and the other teachers. She conquered the demoralizing loneliness of the mission field. She acquired enough of a business sense to realize that charging a tuition fee of fifty cents a month and having a teacher of music in the school who could play a piano or organ made the educational commitment not only more binding, but also more attractive to both students and parents.

Anna Marie was more successful than some other teachers in relating to her students and their parents, in part because of her own rural background. She had grown to maturity on farms in upstate New York and could readily identify with the rural lifestyle of the Hispanic families. As a single woman, she also may have subconsciously seen villagers as her surrogate family.

Enrollment in the Costilla/Garcia school had increased slightly over the previous year to an average of twenty-one students during the first three months of the term, November through January 1883. This increase occurred despite severe epidemics of both diphtheria and typhoid fever that brought death to between twenty and thirty children in the village, including three of the five children of Anna Marie's landlord.

"His oldest daughter, Beatrice, was one of my brightest pupils," she later wrote. Anna Marie and Gilchrist were teaching together for a portion of that year.

The Pueblo Presbytery committed itself to render additional financial support for schools, and the Reverend T. C. Kirkwood, the new superintendent of Colorado Missions who was undoubtedly influenced by Anna Marie, committed his wholehearted support to the endeavor. Furthermore, *The Rocky Mountain Presbyterian*, which was founded by Rev. Sheldon Jackson, continued to do its best to stimulate more financial support from other Presbyterians across the country. This shift in their mission must have been shared by others like J. J. Gilchrist and John G. Reid, her supervisors.

Finally, the Presbytery embraced what the teachers had known all along, that teaching, not preaching, was the first priority; and that Presbyterians could not reach the adult Hispanic population through head-to-head competition with priests.

Anna Marie reported on the journey she made from Costilla/Garcia to Conejos to attend the first meeting of the Pueblo Presbytery held in Conejos in January 1883. She traveled with Gilchrist by wagon, which they rented for one dollar a day. They sat on a "rather rickety spring seat" in the middle of the wagon during the journey. Her report also reveals her excitement about the meeting, her gifts of expression, and the beginning of a more ecumenical view toward Mormons.

> [Upon arrival, we were] assigned to a Mormon family, as there were only two Presbyterian [ladies] in the place, and their houses were full to overflowing. All members of the presbytery visited

more or less the Mexican Protestant families in the vicinity, and, it need hardly be said, were made heartily welcome to all their hosts could offer, and it was by no means poor fare, for when these people became Protestant, it's the letting in of great light for them in things temporal, as well as things spiritual . . . it was my first opportunity for partaking of the Communion with any of our Mexican believers, as my mission work has all been done in plazas where all were Romanists, except the little "vacation teaching" in plaza Manzanares Costilla in which I have been engaged the last summer. To me, it was a day never to be forgotten; Mexicans and Americans, side by side, at the table of the Lord; Mexican elders assisting in the distribution of the elements, and at the close, all joining in the singing of "Nearer My God to Thee," the Spanish words, "Mas Cerca Mi Dios a Ti," blending harmoniously with English rendering that it was all one tongue, the thought came to me, all one in Christ Jesus.

On the way home after the meeting, Anna Marie and Gilchrist stopped over to visit with Effie Miller, the teacher at Cenicero. Traveling between villages was so difficult that despite starving for companionship, teachers seldom visited one another.

Although the teachers' focus was shifting from winning souls to improving literacy, the effort to establish Presbyterian churches in the San Luis Valley continued. In 1883, Episcopal Bishop John F. Spaulding built a small parsonage in Alamosa. By 1885, a missionary preacher, Reverend Honeyman, was visiting Villa Grove, Saguache, Del Norte, and La Jara, where a log chapel was built. By 1889, churches were erected in both Alamosa and La Jara. All these mission churches, however, were established to reach Anglo-American farmers and ranchers, not Hispanics. And with the one exception noted, they operated no schools for Hispanic children. Nevertheless, they provided a spur of competition to the Presbyterians to establish schools.

In May 1883, Anna Marie reported that the little Presbyterian church in Costilla/Garcia, the first in the county, was "doing fairly well this winter. Some three weeks since two men, one of them a 'Penitente' and quite aged, united with our church. Soon after our lay-evangelist [Albert] Jacobs received a letter threatening his life if he remained in the place another week. He replied by holding extra meetings." The Reverend J. J. Gilchrist, undoubtedly with the help of Anna Marie and Colporteur Albert Jacobs had just organized this church in May of 1882, with sixteen members. During the summer of 1883, Anna Marie took a trip back to Kilbourne, Ohio, near Columbus, where she had been living when she was commissioned as a teacher five years earlier. While there, she visited her blind brother Lank and other relatives, called on old friends, and sought additional financial support for her mission school. That fall she and Gilchrist also organized a school in the New Mexico section of Costilla/Garcia at the request of "Romanists."

Anna Marie was still in the Colorado section of Costilla/Garcia in 1884 and was the Costilla County delegate to the Colorado Sabbath School Association. In March of that year, the *Presbyterian Home Missionary* reported that at Costilla/Garcia she had "been set upon by Romanists and had been interfered with by the Methodists [from Mesita], but she [was] overcoming opposition and prospering." This Methodist interference could have come from Padre Alejandro Marchand, a Catholic priest who converted to Methodism and opened a night school for adults in Costilla/Garcia the following year. In any event, Methodists were the first Protestants to preach in Costilla/Garcia and were the only Protestant competition the Presbyterians encountered in their efforts in the valley. Although the Presbyterian focus shifted to literacy, there remained a motivation to prevail against other faith groups.

By then, it was also clear to the Reverend Eneas McLean that, "Our schools have created a demand for schools. Two young Mexicans taught in our schools are now awaiting examination to become teachers in the public schools. In some parts, a sentiment in favor of education has been created strong enough to maintain public schools in the face of the bitter hostility of the Jesuits."

Still later, in March 1884, Reverend McLean reiterated in the *Presbyterian Home Missionary* that the mission schools had created a demand for public schools. In the same issue of the *Presbyterian Home Missionary* March 1884, the Reverend O. E. Boyd reinforced McLean's views by stating that the opportunity had never been greater to open schools for Hispanics because their desire for education was awakening.

A month later, in April 1884, Reverend Boyd reported on the school at Costilla/Garcia.

> Miss A. M. Ross had been teaching [there] . . . for a few years past. Last year Miss Gilchrist assisted her for a time. The work has succeeded so well under her wise administration that she now asks for a permanent assistant; she is thirty-five miles from the nearest minister or teacher. We did not see her school, as we arrived at dusk in the evening, and left next morning. Meanwhile we had a good

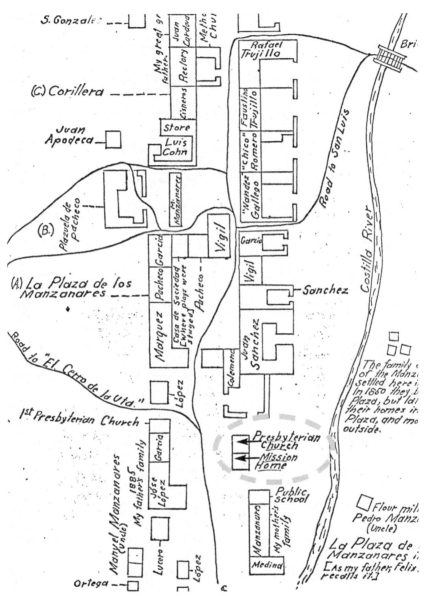

Costilla/Garcia. Note Presbyterian church and mission home.

long council about the field, and also bought a building near Plaza Manzaneros for the double purpose of school and church, for which we paid the great sum of $40.00.

The title to this two-room house was placed in Anna Marie's name. The April 1884 minutes of the Pueblo Presbytery show that it voted to ask the Board of Home Missions for an assistant for her to "labor in [the] Plaza adjoining Miss Ross' school."

According to the Colorado State Census, in June of 1885 Anna Marie had a seventeen-year-old girl from Virginia and an eighteen-year-old from Colorado living with her as boarders. At that time, she, along with Miss Barlow—who had been recruited by Anna Marie and was operating schools both at San Rafael/Mogote and Conejos—requested that a boarding school be established at Costilla/Garcia. There also was a public school in the village taught by Manuel Vigil and a total of 102 students resided in the village, divided about equally between the two schools. That year, the Methodists also opened a school for adults. Albert Jacobs, the colporteur, was a resident and reported his occupation as preacher.

The question was whether the joint request for two teachers—one to assist Anna Marie and a second for a boarding school—should be answered. "Success has attended their day schools," noted the Reverend J. W. Sanderson, "but much, very much more could be done for their permanent good. One of the great lacks of the Mexican women is a lack of knowledge of housekeeping."

That summer, Anna Marie took one of her few vacations, to visit her mother and two brothers and their families in West Virginia. Lank and his wife had moved from Ohio to West Virginia since her last visit with him. Most likely she also sought additional financial support on this trip to pay the salary of the assistant she had been seeking for three years. In any event, by the 1886-87 school year Stella Brengle (from Hanover, Indiana) was assigned as an assistant to Anna Marie, "who felt keenly the need of help in her work." As they were doing for Anna Marie, the Syracuse Presbytery must have paid her salary. In 1886, it raised $2,500.

Except for a short period when Gilchrist assisted her, Anna Marie had worked in Costilla/Garcia alone and was convinced that there was "a greater need of a mission school in the New Mexico side than in the Colorado side of this town." However, she also noted that she "could never consent to have this school [Costilla/Garcia] abandoned while the people are doing their part to keep it up. If there is no other way to have a school in both places, Miss Brengle and I have agreed to separate temporarily."

Rarely one to complain about her health, Anna Marie added, "in view of my tendency to break down under extra pressure, I feel it would not be a very wise decision [to separate us] in the end."

Her concern about her health was apparently ignored. That winter a severe snowstorm isolated Costilla/Garcia for a week, with the snowdrifts blocking doors and windows. It could only have aggravated her condition even further, since she was completely isolated until the accumulated snow could be cleared.

During the next school year, 1887-1888, Brengle wrote that the outlook for the year in the New Mexico school was good. "Already two families, who have not had children in the school before, are sending to us and seem interested. A Roman Catholic came into the room a few mornings since with his little son, whom he wished to place in the school. He remained during the usual devotional exercises. I almost expected to see him take his boy and go; but instead he seemed quite interested, and stayed while he heard two or three classes recite."

In 1887, the Reverend Francis M. Gilchrist (brother of J. J. Gilchrist) visited Costilla/Garcia and reported that "the school work there is in an encouraging condition. An intelligent Mexican tells me that there is a growing sentiment in favor of Protestantism on this field." He also preached there through an interpreter, probably Anna Marie.

As the teachers focused more on literacy, the church hierarchy persisted in the belief that they could ultimately win Catholic souls through schools. By 1887, the *Home Mission Monthly* observed, "During the last few years many schools have been founded and much good has resulted; and while the work is most hopeful, Protestants must establish schools and maintain more churches, or turn the children and youth of the entire population over to the influence of the Catholic Church." The 1888 annual report of the Board of Home Missions noted that missionaries were calling for schools to pave the way for missionary activity to Indians, Hispanics, and Mormons. It noted that these populations "must be reached, if at all, through their children."

Whether their motives were the conversion of Catholics or the reduction of illiteracy, the Syracuse Presbytery raised almost $3,200 in 1888 to support Anna Marie and other missionary efforts.

Financial support notwithstanding, it was proving difficult for the Pueblo Presbytery to retain teachers in the San Luis Valley. By 1888, Anna Marie had been teaching for ten years, persevering in spite of her declining health, but a number of her fellow teachers had given up. That year, the *Home Mission Monthly* noted there had been a large number of changes in the home missionary field because of ill health.

"Owing to the nature of the work, it is very trying physically and mentally, and a few years of faithful service compel one after another of your teachers to seek a year of rest," the publication noted. Nonetheless, no provisions were made for ill or retired missionary teachers.

Clearly Anna Marie possessed the same deep commitment to the battle that her brothers displayed during the Civil War and earlier generations of her family had demonstrated. Loneliness, meager living conditions, poor weather, and resistance or outright hostility had not prompted her to abandon the War for Souls.

During the 1889-90 school year Anna Marie and Brengle were transferred temporarily to Antonito, where they taught forty-two day pupils and twelve "boarding scholars" as well as a Sabbath school for the first six months. For the last six months Anna Marie taught seventy students in Costilla/Garcia. On May 19, 1888, Anna Marie had joined the Costilla Presbyterian Church, then transferred her membership to the Antonito church in April 1890. She wrote that they "could find employment for at least four more teachers in this vicinity; still with one more could occupy the field fairly well." The Antonito school was in a building known as the Huntington Seminary adjacent to the First Presbyterian Church. The Cenicero church, school, and parsonage—all under one roof—were closed that year and its congregation merged with Antonito's.

As their "adopted Home Missionary teacher," Anna Marie was still being supported by the Syracuse Women's Missionary Society in 1890, when the Board of Home Missions also asked the Syracuse society to support Tillie Guy. That year the society raised $3,930 to support two teachers and their home missions, compared with $2,500 in 1886.

Around 1891, probably while living in Antonito, Anna Marie adopted Frances Everett, a six-year-old Hispanic girl. Frances had beautiful black hair and eyes. About that time, fellow teacher Ada Wilson had already adopted an eleven-year-old girl. Anna Marie wrote: "I lived alone last winter, but . . . I did not want to try it again this winter . . . I at last found a child to live with me."

Frances was one of seven children in an impoverished farm family in Saguache, about sixty miles north of Antonito. Her Hispanic mother, Josepha Sanchez, died in Saguache about 1887, shortly after the birth of her last child. The father, John Everett—a Civil War veteran—was unable to both operate his rented 320-acre irrigated farm and take care of his six children. He had to find another home for Frances, who was too sickly to attend school regularly. Undoubtedly, the foster child relationship was arranged through Reverend J. J. Gilchrist, who organized the church in Saguache in

Big Brother: Mexican Pete

The oldest brother of Frances Everett, known as "Mexican Pete," was the boxing champion of Crested Butte in 1896 and fought in Gunnison and San Francisco in 1897. On September 8, 1897, a few days before his bout with Billy Woods, the *Cripple Creek Morning Times* published the following quote to stimulate interest: "I want Billy to know I am still on earth and [hope he] is willing to accept my [*sic*] challenge for the $500 purse." He won on a technicality. He also boxed world champion  Jim Jeffries in 1898 in Cripple Creek, as well as Tom Sharkey and Jack Johnson. In 1899 and 1900 he fought in San Diego, Aspen, Creede, Denver, and Cripple Creek. In 1900 he was jailed in Buena Vista for desecrating the American flag

Pete moved to Pueblo in 1919 and opened a boxing gymnasium. He was said to have fed every boxer who came through town. Pete fought his last fight in 1921, as a benefit for flood refugees. While he lost to every leading boxer he fought except one, Mexican Pete was the best heavyweight Hispanic boxer of his day. In his last years, he worked as a steelworker and watchman for the Colorado Steel and Ironworks. Pete died in 1935 in Pueblo.

1881, and his brother F. M. Gilchrist, who organized one in Antonito. In doing so, they solved Anna Marie's problem as well as John Everett's.

Everett was well known and respected in both Saguache and Antonito, where he had lived. He moved to Saguache in about 1867. By 1868 he was elected as the first sheriff of Saguache County by a vote of fifteen to eight and served until at least 1870, the year he married Josepha Sanchez. He also had served as a district road overseer. He rented his farm from Otto Mears in 1872, and bought livestock and equipment with a loan from Mears. Mears lived part-time on his nearby property at that point, and later became known as the Pathfinder of the San Juans for his road- and railroad-building.

In 1891, Anna Marie taught thirty-two day and boarding pupils in Antonito, where the school opened in 1886. She continued until the school was closed due to the changed character of the town, which had become a railroad center with relatively few Hispanic residents. This was the largest teaching load she had carried. Anna Marie was probably helped by Chrissie Gilchrist, who also was in poor health and therefore living with her mother in Antonito. Gilchrist previously had assisted Anna Marie in Costilla/Garcia.

A large influx of "godless" non-Hispanic American railroad construction workers had altered the character of the community. Railroad construction introduced a wage economy, and while construction continued to the south and west, wrote Virginia Simmons, "the workmen sought comfort in an entertainment capital of sorts in Antonito with its unusually high selection of bars and painted ladies lounging in the open doorways of their shacks." Although she had been committed to working in Antonito, as evidenced by her transferring her church membership there, Anna Marie could not function as a missionary school teacher in this environment with so few Hispanic children. For her, Antonito was as "godless" as Mesilla. To this day, the church to which the school was attached still exists.

Alice T. Marshall took over the existing school in San Luis in 1891 and opened a new school in San Pedro in March. Prior to that time the only school in that village was in a private home and attended by children of well-to-do families. Anna Marie succeeded Marshall in San Pedro, and taught twenty-four day pupils in 1892. She transferred her church membership from Antonito back to Costilla/Garcia in February 1892 because there was as yet no church in San Pedro.

In the spring of 1892 she wrote her sister Charlotte that her health was fine although she believed she had asthma. One of the few visitors she had while living there, a Hispanic preacher named Reverend Gabino Rendon, reported that she served very strong coffee.

Dr. Kirkwood visited the San Luis Valley in the spring of 1892 and reported in May that he had visited eight schools taught by seven teachers, one teacher splitting the year between two schools. This was Anna Marie, who arrived in San Pedro, in 1892 where:

> the people had been praying for her return . . . but when she
> came back the small pox was in the plaza . . . when I visited the

school there were eleven in the school . . . two of the pupils had just recovered from this disease. . . . That teacher lives alone in that plaza, not another white face in it save a little girl [Frances] whom she has just adopted; on the Sabbath she conducts a Sabbath school and every now and then she gives the people a Bible reading. . . . Over on the other side of the Valley there is a place where there are a good many liberal Romanists, and they have been inquiring for a school, because five miles away [in San Luis] many years ago, they had one, and the same teacher is in the valley. . . . By permission of the Board she came the first of March [1891] to San Pedro . . . nineteen of the men were there to hear her tell of the Truth before the goods she brought with her were thoroughly unpacked . . . they gave her a house for herself, and her school. Reverend Rendon took care of Frances while Anna made the move from Antonito.

Anne Marie had twenty-seven students in 1893 while living in a one-room residence attached to the school, which operated the entire year and drew students from five villages within a five-mile radius of San Pedro. The sixth Presbyterian church in the valley was opened that year in San Pedro. Organized in association with the school, the church had eighteen founding members, many of whom were recruited by Anna Marie.

In 1893, Anna Marie's last year in a mission school, the San Pedro schoolroom was in a rented adobe building, eighteen by sixty feet, once used as a dance hall. The children brought their own seats, some using boxes. There were no desks, but it was better equipped with instructional materials than the public schools in the area.

The *Home Mission Monthly,* in 1893, observed that New Mexicans were still not ready for Protestant churches unless they were associated with schools:

> Plant a church in a purely Mexican community in New Mexico [or Colorado] and you arouse not only the hostility of the priest but of the people as well; but plant a school in the same community; put at its head a loving, motherly woman [and] she will receive a cordial welcome . . . the priest may threaten excommunication, but the teacher will win, and lay solid . . . foundations for a church.

Villagers willingly incorporated the Anglo women teachers into the framework of village life. And the successful teacher attempted to bring change only within that framework. Clearly, this was the secret of Anna Marie's success.

Anna Marie retired in September 1893. The Pueblo Presbytery noted in its minutes that she was "obliged to withdraw from active service on account of impaired health." Finally diagnosed as having tuberculosis, she made an application for aid and was "allowed by the Board the sum of $130 for one year." Presumably this covered the rail fare to West Virginia, where she and Frances would live with her brother and his family.

Although Anna Marie believed she had asthma during her years in the San Luis Valley, it is at least possible that tuberculosis had been the cause of her ill health. She had lived in windowless, one-room, dirt-floored adobe houses with a fireplace in one corner as the sole source of heat and the only means of cooking. Judging by her correspondence, she had a constitution strong enough to withstand fifteen bitterly cold, long winters without complaint and with more success than most of the ministers and lady teachers.

In all of Anna Marie's correspondence during her fifteen-year period of service that has been preserved, she commented only twice about ill health, referring to her "asthmatic condition," which actually must have been tuberculosis contracted during her first winter there. In the other case she noted she had "a tendency to break down under any extra pressure." And only on two occasions did she indicate dissatisfaction with her supervisor (Reverend Darley), and never about her fellow "soldiers."

She had apparently outlasted all her colleagues in the San Luis Valley. Because of the nature of the work, the isolation and loneliness, bitter winter weather, and exposure to contagious diseases, most of the teachers sought a rest after several years of this service, if it were within their means to do so. There were no provisions for disabled or retired missionary teachers. This was true despite the fact that one of the functions of the Woman's Board of Home Missions was "to secure aid and comfort for home missionaries and missionary laborers in special cases of affliction and destitution."

During Anna Marie's fifteen years in the Southwest, one teacher found it necessary to return east to wait for spring. The Reverend W. W. Morton, a preacher who arrived in the valley in September 1880 to take up his duties, was gone by the following March, having been completely demoralized by the cold weather. By January he had written: "I am about played out, I am weak . . . have cold all the time."

During this span of fifteen years, 1878-93, Anna Marie taught for eight years in Costilla/Garcia, one of the three double villages that emerged in the San Luis Valley. With Anna Marie's help, a Presbyterian church was opened in Costilla in 1882. San Rafael/Mogote was the second double village. This school, known as the San Juan School, was attached to the church in

Mogote. She ended her career in the third, San Pablo-San Pedro. In each of these dual towns, one community was Catholic and one Protestant and they were still divided religiously as late as 1924.

Susie Grimstead, teaching in the San Luis school during the year that Anna Marie was in Mesilla, could not attract students and became so disheartened that she asked for a transfer. Later, Anna Marie also taught in Antonito, where neither Lexie Barlow, nor Stella Brengle, nor Ada Wilson (who was from Greencastle, Indiana) could attract Hispanic children to the school. Barlow was not physically strong enough to carry on her work. Anna Marie also was unsuccessful there but for other reasons.

Unlike most of the other teachers, Anna Marie usually took no vacation in the summer, although occasionally she took a short one. For example, in 1880, the summer she went to Mesilla, she took only a month's vacation because she "feared some time might elapse before another teacher should reach [San Luis]." This commitment to the Protestant work ethic also led her to spend many summers engaged in "vacation work" which consisted of traveling to nearby villages and *placitas* to recruit students for the next term and to conduct Bible readings in Spanish in the plazas. Still other summers she visited friends and relatives in New York and Ohio to raise funds to pay her salary and that of at least one other teacher.

Her last year in the valley, 1893, was the year that the Presbyterian Board of Home Missions concluded there were five hindrances to its missionary work. One of these clearly suggests that the board had learned what the front line troops had long recognized: attempting to convert Hispanics by evangelical missionary work bore very little fruit.

> The fourth hindrance is the machinations of the Jesuits. They had a missionary in nearly every nursery in our large towns and cities, and a representative in every legislative assembly. They seek to exert the combined influence of the mitre, the purse, and the sword. Their strategy and their tactics are arranged for the South and the great West. In many cases, their pioneers are political agitators, and their priests demagogues. They are in alliance with crowned heads and command the gold of princes to further their enterprises. They are seeking to gain in the New World the power they have lost in the Old.

With the full support of Jackson, Kendall, and Roberts, she had thrown herself whole-heartedly into a full-scale war against illiteracy shortly after her arrival. She was as loyal to this cause as she was to her family and to what she regarded as the true faith, Covenanting Scots Reformed Presbyterianism. To her, religion and education went hand in hand, a basic tenet of the Covenanting Presbyterians. Nevertheless, it did not take her long to reverse her priorities.

It is clear that she started out to evangelize by teaching; she ended up teaching as a means to evangelize. This transformation undoubtedly explains much of her disagreement with Alex Darley. She had been in the valley long enough to learn the cultural values of the Hispanic villages rather than attempt to change them. The correspondence from the mission field also reveals that the other teachers, all of whom were younger, accepted her judgments regarding matters about which she felt strongly—teaching music, having teachers work in pairs wherever possible, opening boarding schools for girls, teaching adults, teaching Sunday School, and teaching the Bible in the plazas. Finally, the correspondence reveals that she was an ardent admirer of both Jackson and Kendall, as were they of her.

In addition to evangelizing and establishing churches over a period of fifteen years from 1878 to 1893, the Presbyterian Church opened a total of approximately thirty mission schools for Hispanics, sixteen of which were in southern Colorado, the balance in New Mexico. It located six of these in Costilla and Conejos counties, including three in double villages: Costilla/Garcia, San Rafael/Mogote, and San Pedro/San Pablo. The other three were Antonito, Conejos, and San Luis. During this fifteen-year period, Anna Marie Ross taught in all of the six schools in these two counties and one in New Mexico. In common with other Protestant churches by then, the Presbyterians were learning that only through the children could they make a lasting impression on their Hispanic parents.

Anna Marie and her handful of fellow missionary teachers in southern Colorado had only one practical advantage. As the *Home Mission Monthly* noted, "Evangelists and missionaries found difficulty in gaining access to them [Hispanics] . . . The lady teacher [however] is welcome at homes where the Protestant minister is regarded with suspicion." On the other hand the more effective the teacher, the more she threatened the power of the priest. The trust and friendship of the Hispanic parents had to be won. Within the Native American population, the missionary school teachers had the further advantage of three centuries of hostility between the Mexican Americans, who considered themselves primarily Hispanic, and those Native Americans (principally Utes, Apaches, and Navajos) who often chafed under traditional Mexican hegemony. However, Anna Marie and her colleagues were disadvantaged in the Hispanic community. The Hispanics were loyal to Catholicism and to the Spanish language, which they spoke with re-

John Everett and his three daughters, including Frances, who is not individually identified.

Photo courtesy of Saguache Historical Museum

markable purity, as a result of two and a half centuries of domination.

The Presbyterian missionary efforts of Anna Marie and others who learned the Spanish language helped to break down racial barriers in the valley and a few of their Hispanic converts were ordained as evangelists, elders, and ministers. To train these converts, the Presbyterian College of the Southwest was established. The anti-Catholicism of Presbyterians who were competing to establish missions, schools, and churches among Spanish-speaking Roman Catholics clearly motivated this effort. Presbyterians viewed Catholicism as the "oppression of a heartless and despotic church that has kept the Mexicans this long in ignorance and poverty, and is fast ripening the fields of harvest for the Protestant sickle." Mission schools brought together Hispanics and Anglos in an atmosphere of mutual acceptance and appreciation of each other's cultural background. They also filled the void created by the absence of public schools.

By 1902, the Woman's Board of Home Missions concluded that the missionary teacher was "the unordained, untitled, unheralded, womanly wedge that inserts the gospel under the crust of heathen ignorance, till the break is made which admits the church and the minister."

By the end of 1893 Anna Marie had moved into the Hedgesville, West Virginia, home of her brother, Dr. Daniel Reid Ross, a country doctor. She was sixty-two. Her brother did all he could to treat her medically with what was then known as the best care for tuberculosis. The only possessions she brought with her from Colorado were a tightly woven Ute Indian basket, her prized silverware, and long-stemmed tulip glasses. From the $7,500 she had earned—$500 annually for 15 years with no raises—she loaned her brother money interest-free to help finance construction of the only house he ever owned.

She had arrived in Hedgesville with Frances Everett, by then nine years old. Frances stayed with her until about 1900, when she returned to Saguache to live on a small farm with her father and two sisters. There, she completed her high school education in a building that now houses the Saguache Historical Museum.

Anna Marie's patience, courage, and fortitude were to be tested severely by bodily suffering for the last eleven years of her life. She continued to teach Sunday school in the local Reformed Presbyterian Church. When she knew her death was near, she ordered her coffin made to her design by the local cabinetmaker. She died in 1904 and is buried in the churchyard of the second oldest Scots Reformed Presbyterian church west of the Blue Ridge Mountains. She left her very small estate to her brother and forgave the loan she had made to him.

EIGHT

— ⋅ —

Outcomes of the War for Souls

Because of limited financial resources and the fact that many Presbyterians agreed with the concept of state control of education, the church, after the Civil War, limited its efforts to establishing mission schools among "exceptional populations," particularly including such non-English-speaking people as Hispanics and Native Americans. Many of these schools closed as public schools opened.

In the case of the San Luis Valley, Anna Marie Ross undoubtedly encouraged two of her neighbors in Costilla/Garcia, C.J. Brickenstein and Dr. Joseph Kugler, to become public school superintendents of Conejos and Costilla counties. Brickenstein created seven new school districts during his two-year term of office. Thus, the rise of public schools contributed to the demise of Presbyterian missionary schools, partly because of her influence on these two men.

In her fifteen years of uninterrupted service, as well as her relationship with Brickenstein and Kugler, Anna Marie paved a large part of the way toward a public elementary and secondary school system in the San Luis Valley.

We cannot quantify her impact but, with one exception, it is a far more onerous task even to identify other forces that might have contributed to the emergence of public schools during the period she was in the valley. Specifically, the efforts of Horace Mann and countless other educators over the three decades of 1865-1895, to gain more and more popular support for state control of elementary education was felt even in the San Luis Valley, remote though it was from mainstream America. How to measure the impact of Mann's educational philosophy in the valley is another question.

Virtually the only local forces advocating free public education were the Presbyterian mission schools and the Mormons who provided them with a "spur of competition" while Anna Marie and the other eighteen teachers were on the scene. No schools had been funded by either the Spanish or the Mexican governments prior to annexation by the United States. During this period and for much longer, the Spanish tradition of education as a privilege of well-to-do families largely prevailed. Neither before nor after annexation—with one exception in Conejos—had the Catholic Church supported public schooling in the San Luis Valley. When southern Colorado came under territorial government, Congress did nothing to fund schools there or in any other territory. And in the early years of the office, the superintendent of public instruction of Colorado took no action except to bemoan the lack of local financial support for public schools.

While Colorado was still a territory, a number of educators commented on "the deplorable state of affairs in the southern counties with their Spanish-speaking population." In 1871, the Colorado superintendent of public instruction noted that caste either prevented admission of Hispanic children to public schools, or they were kept ignorant of their educational privileges, or no inducements were held out to them.

In his 1875 report, Horace M. Hale, Colorado superintendent of public instruction, complained that he was unable to obtain reports on school conditions from public officials in Costilla and Conejos counties. "From private sources I learn that the schools in these counties are sadly neglected. Children are plentiful enough, but they are permitted to grow up in utter ignorance. . . . A compulsory law, strictly enforced in this portion of Colorado, would result in good."

Between 1883 and 1890, however, public schools increased in Costilla and Conejos counties from twenty-one to thirty-four, teachers from thirty-nine to seventy-three, and pupils doubled from 1,281 to 2,607. This coincides with the period of greatest activity by the Presbyterian mission schools in these two counties. In the opinion of the Reverend John G. Reid, this growth in public school education also was accelerated by the competitive response of the Catholic churches in villages such as San Luis to open a "sister's school" (1882) in opposition to the Presbyterian mission school, thus awakening "a desire for better educational facilities which erelong will result in a demand for public schools . . . free from strictly denominational control."

Almost a century later, Norman John Bender reflected on Presbyterian efforts in his 1971 doctoral dissertation.

> Certainly another tangible achievement of western Presbyterian missionaries was the result of their educational endeavors. Their own schools were not spectacular successes. . . . But the Presbyterian schools also served as gadflies to local, territorial, and state governing bodies who sometimes appeared to be slothful in their support for continuation in the West of the revered system of widespread and high quality public education facilities.

The mission schools also helped to elevate the standards of the public schools. Mission schools were better equipped with instructional materials and often attracted children from surrounding villages. Their teachers were better paid and trained.

Mission schools not only stimulated the formation of public schools but trained teachers who staffed them. By 1884, the first two graduates of mission schools who wanted to become teachers in public schools were awaiting the opportunity to take the examination. As a result, according to one observer, the Hispanic population of the San Luis Valley had "produced more than [its] quota of teachers, musicians, administrators, lawyers, public officials, and other business and professional men and women." According to another, one southern Colorado public school principal and five of his teachers were alumni of mission schools. Five children from one family who attended the San Rafael/Mogote school became teachers. By the turn of the century, as public schools were established and began meeting educational needs, the Presbyterian mission schools were closed one by one, throughout the San Luis Valley. Anna Marie Ross opened the school in San Luis in 1878. It closed in 1916. The Costilla/Garcia school, also opened in 1878 by Pitts was closed and sold in 1903.

From an analysis of the Costilla County school records spanning the years Anna Marie spent in southern Colorado (1878-1893), we can measure her impact, in combination with other factors, on the public school system. These records reveal that there were no publicly owned school buildings, and no school taxes were levied the year before she arrived. Voluntary donations paid teacher salaries. No school had blackboards, books, wall maps or globes, and none of the teachers spoke Spanish. School terms were as short as two months, attendance was a fraction of the school age population of the county, and at least 90 percent of students as well as of the total population were illiterate.

By 1892, fifteen years later and the last year Anna Marie taught in the village of Costilla/Garcia, where she taught for almost eight years, the school district had built a school and hired a salaried teacher despite the fact that it was among the most impoverished school districts in the county. Its taxes provided only half as much money per pupil as the average for the county as a whole. Further, enrollment in her mission school plus that in the public school had totaled virtually 100 percent of the school-age population for at least five years. Surely this was an achievement few if any rural schools west of the Mississippi River could claim at that time!

The impact of Anna Marie and her colleagues spilled over into the rest of the county. In 1877, the year before she and Pitts arrived, the county school superintendent deemed it "very hard to get even a shadow of compliance with the school laws in the County. Not a single district out of eight in the County having come up to even the broadest interpretation of the school law." He continued, "[I] report no school lands available in the County for school purposes in as much as the whole county seems to belong to the Sangre de Cristo grantees [William Blackmore, the English land speculator, and Dutch bankers who had gone bankrupt and were not paying taxes]."

In his annual report for 1878, the year Anna Marie Ross and Susie Pitts arrived, the Conejos County superintendent remarked, "I am ashamed of this report. . . . Nine tenths of persons between the age of 6 and 21 years in the county are Mexicans and they are apparently taught that 'ignorance is bliss.'" Certainly the Costilla County superintendent would not have disagreed. Yet by 1890 there were sixteen schools in the county with an enrollment of 1,933, two-thirds of the school age population.

In 1878, Costilla County had eight school districts but none owned school houses or collected school taxes. All the schools were ungraded. The superintendent observed in his annual report that in each school district teachers were paid by voluntary contributions but that rent for schools and other expenses could not be met because of the smallpox epidemic and economic distress resulting from four successive years of crop failure.

Not until 1882 were school taxes collected in the county, totaling $2,693.50. That year there were four new school houses owned by school districts and a total of nine school districts organized, utilizing fourteen teachers who earned an average monthly salary of $29.76. The longest operating school district held classes during 189 days, while sixty days was the shortest school year.

This was also the school year that Dr. Joseph Kugler, Anna Marie's neighbor, was the county superintendent. He had previously served four one-year terms on the San Luis Village school board. In his annual report for 1884, the superintendent further noted, "[It] is almost a necessity in this county to have teachers well versed in the Spanish language so that they may be better enabled to teach English." He based that statement in part on his visit in February 1884 to the Costilla/Garcia village public school where Julian Beall was the teacher. The superintendent's report of that visit noted, "pupils learning English were dull. The reason for that may be in the fact that the pupils do very rarely hear English spoken outside of the school."

Between 1885 and 1889 the superintendent reported on his difficulties in collecting full and complete information from various districts needed to compile his annual reports.

The year of 1889 also marked the first time a school district in the county sold a bond issue ($2,000). Twelve schools owned textbooks that year in comparison with five the previous year.

Not until 1891 did Costilla County begin operation of its first graded school. By then there were twenty-one school districts in the county operating sixteen schools with seventeen teachers. Every school had wall maps and blackboards but only twelve owned textbooks. The district spent an average of $2.64 per student in 1884; by 1891, it had increased to $4.10 per student. In that same period, the number of teachers increased from twelve to seventeen, and their salaries went from $29.76 to $45 per month.

Three school bond issues totaling $7,930 had been sold in 1893, Anna Marie's last year. By then, there were twenty-five teachers in twenty schools with an average daily attendance of 545, more than a third of the school-age population.

Three of the public schools—six of the teachers and 270 of the pupils, half of the total—were in three Costilla County villages where Anna Marie had taught: San Luis, Costilla/Garcia, and San Pablo. All school bonds were retired so that average monthly expenditure per pupil dropped from $4.50 to $2.87. The graded school, however, was no longer operating.

During this timespan of fifteen years, 1878-93, 1892 was the year the county school superintendent seemed the most optimistic. In his annual report, he stated that some encouragement could be drawn from comparing 1892 results with previous years. He wrote, "[During the year] we have obtained some teachers who are both able and willing to perform the arduous labor of instruction [and] at this writing the twenty districts . . . are periodically out of debt. The south half of the county is occupied exclusively by Mexicans . . . the less populated districts [were merged] to obtain a more proficient Board of Directors."

Costilla/Garcia was certainly one of the poorest villages in the entire county. In 1892 it had only $1.15 of tax revenue per month per pupil available to spend in its single ungraded school, as compared with $2.87 per pupil for the county as a whole, to spend in the twenty schools reporting that year. Despite this financial handicap, there was virtually 100 percent enrollment of the 162 school-age children in either the public school or Ross's mission school in the village that year. In fact, enrollment had approached 100 percent since 1885. Obviously, how much impact on this record Ross had cannot be measured, but it certainly was significant.

In the course of her fifteen years in the San Luis Valley, Anna Marie Ross founded and/or taught in seven different schools:

> San Luis: October 1878-September 1880; December 1881-1882
> Mesilla: September 1880 to June 1881
> Costilla/Garcia: July 1882-1889
> Costilla and Antonito (half time in each): 1889-1891
> San Pedro: 1892-1893

A further indication of her far-reaching impact can be seen in the large number of church groups in New York that contributed to her work, including Amboy, Baldwinsville, Cazenova, Fayetteville, Jordan, Liverpool, Manlius, Marcellus, Syracuse, Oswego, Camillus, Belle Isle, Constantia, Skaneateles, East Syracuse, Fulton, and Elbridge.

Anna Marie and her eighteen colleagues, however, did not bring victory to the Presbyterians in the War for Souls. The school in San Pedro where she last taught closed in 1916. The others had closed earlier. Although the attached church still survives as the only Presbyterian church in the entire county, its congregation in 1986 numbered only seven, hardly evidence of a major impact. In 1894, the year after she left the valley, there were only nine Presbyterian churches serving the Hispanic population in the entire state. Today, the only Spanish-speaking Presbyterian congregation in the valley is at San Pablo. It was founded in 1885. The school attached to that church is the last one in which she taught.

Today's public school system in the county in large part, however, can be viewed as a monument to the efforts of the Presbyterian missionary school teachers, including Anna Marie Ross. Surely her fifteen-year record reflects a widespread recognition of the value of education to parents and children. And just as surely, this recognition was due in large part to Anna Marie's personal war against illiteracy. Education of children was an end in itself. She proved her skills in teaching the three R's—if not her creed. For her, teaching—not evangelizing—was the primary goal.

In a memoir he wrote in retirement about 1900, Reverend J.J. Gilchrist—who had been one of Anna Marie's supervisors in the 1880s—said, "One of the hardest lessons I have had to repeat over and over was that neither layman nor preacher can win souls just by fighting Romanism."

Anna Marie Ross and her eighteen colleagues also brought together for the first time Hispanics and Anglos in an atmosphere of mutual acceptance and appreciation of each other's cultural backgrounds.

San Pablo Presbyterian Church

EPILOGUE

The relatively remote San Luis Valley today, with its dry climate and parched landscape, remains one of the poorest rural areas in Colorado. Agriculture predominates, although tourism is growing slowly in response to both natural and historic attractions. Unemployment is higher than average and as much as a quarter of the population lives below the poverty line. The majority of the people living there claim Hispanic or Latino heritage, particularly in Costilla and Conejos counties, where Anna Marie lived and worked for fifteen years.

From earliest Hispanic settlement, a bastion of the valley's economy was the right to hunt, fish, harvest timber, and graze their livestock on communal lands, promised to them in a million-acre Mexican land grant. After the land was ceded to the United States, those rights were guaranteed to the original settlers by the Treaty of Guadalupe Hidalgo, which was signed and subsequently ratified by Congress in 1848. Cattle and sheep ranches and subsistence farms growing pinto beans, potatoes, chilies, corn, and alfalfa all depended on irrigation water from snow melting in the high country.

As outsiders sought ways to profit from the vast open lands in the valley and surrounding mountains in the late 1800s, there were innumerable conflicts over those rights. Hispanic sheepherders and Anglo cattlemen clashed, creating a wave of violence and terrorism that drove many Hispanics from the valley by the mid-1890s. As the speculators went broke, the Travelers Insurance Company began to acquire, by purchase or expropriation, additional thousands of acres adjacent to land it already controlled, in order to utilize the vast irrigation network fed by the headwaters of the Rio Grande. Despite this population exodus in the 1880s and 1890s, the sheep population of Conejos and Costilla counties doubled from 100,000 to 200,000, thanks to summer grazing in the Sangre de Cristo Mountains.

The population of Costilla County peaked in 1940 at about 7,500. Still, the Great Depression and related drought had hit the area hard. In the following decade, people left—an outmigration that is still felt today, with fewer than half the number of residents recorded in 1940.

An even more devastating blow hit the people of Costilla County in 1960. Unlike its neighbors, Costilla County has no federal lands. The communal lands of their ancestors were critical to their ability to raise crops and livestock, to hunt for food, and to harvest the timber needed for homes and ranches. But in that year, North Carolina timber baron Jack Taylor bought 77,500 of those acres. As the title was transferred to him, he was told by authorities to expect trouble from the local people, many of whom were descendants of the original colonists. In response, he fenced the entire 121 square miles and hired gunmen to patrol the fences to keep out those he regarded as trespassers. By 1961, a violent feud started when Taylor's gunslingers severely beat three Hispanics he suspected of setting fire to one of his ranch trailers.

Taylor and his ranch hands were taken into custody to protect them from 200 angry residents who threatened to lynch them. In 1965, Taylor won a lawsuit clearing his deed of the language that allowed community use of his ranch. Residents watched helplessly as Douglas-fir and Ponderosa pines were stripped from the land, and streams were dammed, curtailing the flow of water into valley irrigation ditches. Shootouts, vandalism, fires, and cattle rustling persisted until a bullet ripped through Taylor's house and hit him in the ankle. Taylor moved back to his North Carolina home.

In 1981, the case took another legal turn when 150 residents filed a class action lawsuit arguing that descendants of the original settlers were denied due process by Taylor's 1965 lawsuit. They appealed court rulings against them. After Taylor's death in 1988, his son Jackson took over. He put the property up for sale and continued logging, despite demonstrators' attempts to block the trucks at ranch entrances. In 1995, a mysterious fire destroyed the ranch house.

By 1997, no one had stepped forward to buy the ranch. Since 1960, when Taylor bought the ranch, 20 million board feet of lumber had been cut, negatively affecting the land's value. One forestry expert estimated it would take 200 to 500 years for the logged areas to recover. Taylor lowered his asking price to $20,000,000. Then-Governor Roy Romer attempted unsuccessfully to pool public and private funds, and offered to purchase the ranch for $12,000,000, the appraised value, then turn it into a public park, and restore the community rights of the descendants of the original setters.

Taylor sold the land to a high-ranking Enron executive in 1997. Five years later, the Colorado Supreme Court overturned the 1965 ruling that barred descendants of the original Hispanic settlers from the ranch property. They would not be allowed to hunt, fish, or recreate on the land, but would have "rights of access for grazing, firewood, and timber."

The ranch was sold again in 2004, for $60 million, to a group of Texas ranchers who re-named it "Cielo Vista." They bought it with the intention of managing the land as a private elk hunting preserve. In early 2017, the owners put the ranch back on the market, asking $105 million. In August 2017, Texas oil heir William Bruce Harrison bought it. Preliminary reports from the brokerage handling the sale asserted that Harrison would "not be developing it . . . other than fixing it up and maintaining it and being very involved in stewarding that property." A third of the ranch's 83,368 acres are in a conservation easement.

The *Denver Post* reported in March 2017 that more than 500 people are deemed descendants of the Spanish and Mexican settlers on the original land grant. The court ruling restored to all of them the right to graze livestock, gather firewood, and cut timber on the ranch.

Through their efforts to improve literacy and establish the foundations for public schools in the San Luis Valley, Anna Marie Ross and her compatriots made an enduring impact. When they arrived in the valley, inhabitants were illiterate, and minimally equipped to fight for the guarantees made to them in the original land grants. The teachers' legacy of literacy and education paved the way for descendants of those colonists to assert and ultimately reclaim their rights.

REFERENCES

Ahlstrom, Sydney E. *A Religious History of the American People.* New Haven: 1972.

Alamosa Valley Courier, "Cielo Vista ranch owner revealed," September 25, 2017.

Alsberg, Henry, ed., *New Mexico,* American Guide Series. New York, 1973.

An Historical Sketch of the Synod of Colorado, undated pamphlet.

Annin, Rev. John. *Revista Evangelica,* July 1877.

Annual Reports, 1878-1893; and Record Book of Costilla County School Superintendent, 1871-1892, Colorado State Archives, Denver, Colorado.

Anthearn, Frederic J. "Land of Contrast: A History of Southeast Colorado," *BLM Cultural Resources Series* (Colorado No. 17), 1985.

Arrington, Leonard J. *Great Basin Kingdom.* Cambridge: 1958.

_____, *The Mormon Experience.* Chicago: 1992.

Bailey, Alvin Keith. *The Strategy of Sheldon Jackson in Opening the West for National Missions,* Ph.D. Thesis, Yale University, 1948.

Banker, Mark A. "They Made History Slowly," American Presbyterian, Vol. 69, No. 2,Summer 1991, pp. 124-129.

Barber, Ruth K. and Edith J. Agnew, *Sowers Went Forth.* Albuquerque: 1971.

Barley, George M. *Pioneering in the San Juan.* New York: 1899.

Barnes, Albert. *Rocky Mountain Presbyterian,* January 28, 1874.

Bean, Luther. *Land of the Blue Sky People.* Alamosa, CO: 1972.

Bender, Norman John. *The Crusade of the Blue Banner; Rocky Mountain Presbyterianism, 1870-1900,* Ph.D. Thesis, University of Colorado, 1971.

Berwekh, Sister Edward Mary. "John Baptiste Salponte, 1825-1894," *New Mexico Historical Review,* Vol. 37, No. 2. Santa Fe: April 1962.

Billington, Ray. *The Protestant Crusade.* New York: 1938.

Blackmore, William. *Investments in Land in Colorado and New Mexico,* 1876 (privately printed).

Blackmore, William Papers, #0148-0151 and #0130-0130, New Mexico State Records Center and Archives, Santa Fe, New Mexico.

_____ Papers, #0511.

_____ Papers, #0098-0099.

Blackmore, William. *The Spanish-Mexican Land Grants,* Vol. I. Denver: 1949.

Blake, Alice. Unpublished *Memoirs,* pp. 103-104 (copy in author's files).

Blevins, Jason. "With high-end real estate sales on the rebound, an iconic ranch in San Luis Valley is offered for $105 million," *Denver Post,* March 18, 2017.

_____. "Cielo Vista Ranch — and its fourteener — in San Luis Valley sells after listing for $105 million," *Denver Post,* August 14, 2017.

Board of Home Missions. *Annual Reports for 1892.*

_____, *Annual Report,* 1888.

Boyd, Lois A. and R. Douglas Brackenridge, *Presbyterian Women in America.* Westport, CT: 1983.

Brackenridge, R. Douglas. *Iglesia Presbyteriana.* San Antonio: 1974.

Brayer, Herbert O. *William Blackmore: The Spanish-Mexican Land Grants,* Vol. I. Denver: 1949.

Breck, Allen du Pont. *The Episcopal Church in Colorado.* Denver: 1963.

Buchanan, Rosemary. *The First 100 Years – St. Genevieve's Parish 1859-1959.* (n.d.).

Buck, Lucius E. *An Inquiry into the History of Presbyterian Historical Missions,* M.A. Thesis, University of Southern California, 1949).

Campa, Arthur L. *Hispanic Culture in the Southwest.* Norman, Oklahoma: 1979.

Chavez, Angelico. *My Penitente Land.* Albuquerque: 1974.

Christian Observer. Louisville: April 13, 1904.

Colorado Magazine of History, Vol. 55, No. 2, Spring-Summer 1958.

_____, Vol. 52, No. 1, winter 1975, p. 35.

Combs, D. Gene. *Enslavement of Indians in the San Luis Valley of Colorado,* M.A. Thesis, Adams State College, Alamosa, Colorado, 1970.

Colorado State Census of 1885, Colorado State Archives, Denver, Colorado.

Cooper, Arthur B. *The Story of Our Presbytery, 1870-1950.* Denver: 1950 (pamphlet.

Costilla County School Superintendent, Annual Reports, 1878-93, Colorado State Archives.

Curtin, Dave. "Home again, but it's changed," *Denver Post,* August 7, 2005.

Darley, A.M. Del Norte, Colorado, January 26, 1877, SJL-7-8.

Deutsch, Sarah. *No Separate Refuge.* New York: 1987.

Eighteenth Annual Report of the Board of Home Missions, General Assembly of the Presbyterian Church.

Espinosa, J. Manuel. "The Neapolitan Jesuits on the Colorado Frontier, 1868-1919," *Colorado Magazine of History* (Denver), Vol. 15 No. 1, January 1938, p. 67.

Family correspondence (in author's file).

Faris, D.S. "The Covenantor Church in the Civil War," *The Christian Nation,* Vol. 55, October 4, 1911.

Flower, Jr., Judson H. *Mormon Colonization of the San Luis Valley, Colorado, 1878-1900,* M.A. Thesis, Brigham Young University, 1966.

Folks and Fortunes, Sagas of the San Luis V alley, Vol. 1, No. 1, November 1, 1949, p. 70.

Fourth and Seventh Biennial Reports of the Superintendent of Public Instruction, State of Colorado, Costilla and Conejos Counties, Colorado State Archives, Denver, Colorado.

Fuller, Timothy, ed. *Diary of the Jesuit Residence of Our Lady of Guadalupe Parish Church, Conejos, Colorado, December 1871-December 1875* (Colorado Springs 1982).

General Assembly of the Presbyterian Church, *Reports of the Boards,* 1890.

_____, Reports of the Boards, 1893.

General Catalogue, Presbyterian Theological Seminary (Chicago, 1939), p. 86

General Laws, State of Colorado, 1877, Chapter 2473, Sections 27-30.

_____, Chapter 146, Section 105, pp. 815-816.

Gibson, Jr., C.E., recorder, "Settlements and Roads in the San Luis Valley," *Colorado Writers' Project,* WPA.

Gilchrist, J.J. "Ten Years," *J.J. Gilchrist Papers,* Menaul School Historical Library (Albuquerque, no date)

_____, "Memoirs," (undated) Menaul Historical Society, Albuquerque, New Mexico.

Goodykoontz, Colin Brummitt. *Home Missions of the American Frontier.* Caldwell, Idaho: 1939.

Grantor Index 1882-1885, *Costilla County Land Records* (San Luis, Colorado), pp. 442-443.

Guild, Thelma S. and Harvey L. Carter, *Kit Carson.* Lincoln, Nebraska: 1984.

Harris, Elsie Sanchez [sister of Josephine Sanchez], correspondence dated October 15, 1990.

Hastings, S.J., Martin F. *Parochial Beginnings in Colorado to 1889,* M.A. Thesis, St. Louis University, 1941.

Historical Records Survey (Costilla County), Inventory of the County Archives of Colorado, No. 25, WPA.

Historical Records Survey (Conejos County), Inventory of the County Archives of Colorado, No. 11, WPA.

"History of the Presbyterian Church of Cenicero, Conejos County, Colorado," *Minutes of the Session, Cenicero Presbyterian Churches,* Book 2 (n.d.), photocopy in author's possession.

Hoffman's Catholic Directory. Milwaukee: 1878.

Home Mission Monthly, Vol. 5, 1892-93, p. 129.

Interviews in Alamosa, Conejos, Costilla and Rio Grande Counties, *Colorado Writers' Project,* WPA, C.E. Gibson, Recorder, Colorado Historical Society, Denver.

Jackson, Sheldon, 1834-1909, *Correspondence Collection,* Presbyterian Historical Society.

Jackson, Sheldon Scrapbook Collection, Vols. 40, 41, Presbyterian Historical Society.

_____, letter by Alexander M. Darley dated Aug. 19, 1880, Vol. 40.

Jessen, Kenneth. "Colorado's Oldest Occupied Settlement," *Colorado Central Magazine*, Oct. 1, 2010, CoZine.com.

Jones, Oakah L. "Hispanic Traditions and Improvisations of the Frontier of New Spain," *New Mexico Historical Review* (Santa Fe), 56:4, 1981.

Jones, William H. *The History of Catholic Education in the State of Colorado.* Washington DC: 1955.

Journal of the West, July 1980, pp. 26-37.

Kansas City Bulletin. Kansas City, Missouri: n. d.

Lambert, Ruth E. *The Wooden Canvas: Arborglyphs of Hispano Life Along the Pine-Piedra Stock Driveway.* San Juan Mountains Association, Durango, Colorado: 2014.

Lantis, David W. *The San Luis Valley: Sequent Rural Occupance in an Intermountain Basin*, Ph.D. Thesis, Ohio State University, Columbus, 1950.

Las Cruces Sun News, February 22, 1976.

Los Angeles Times, November 17, 1993.

MacLeod, M.H. *Historical Sketch of the Presbytery of Pueblo.* Pueblo, CO: 1906.

Manchester Guardian. Manchester, United Kingdom: August 13, 1873.

Marsh, Charles S. *People of the Shining Mountains.* Boulder, Colorado: 1982.

Martin, Bernice, ed. Frontier Eyewitness: Diary of John Lawrence. Saguache County Museum; Denver: 1990.

Maxwell, Grant. "Course of Empire," *New Mexico,* Vol. 16, No. 10, October 1938.

Mcbride, Peter. "Chaos Comes to Costilla County," *High Country News*, June 9, 1997.

McLean, Robert N. *Spanish and Mexican in Colorado.* New York: 1924.

Mead, Frances Harvey. *Conejos County 1884.* Colorado Springs: 1984.

Mesilla News. Mesilla, New Mexico: August 14, 1881.

Minutes of the Presbytery of Colorado, Vol. II, 1878-1880.

Minutes of the Women's Missionary Society of the Presbytery of Syracuse, 1877-1891 (unpaged), Presbyterian Historical Society.

Montoya, Vivián F. *Silver Threads & Golden Needles: I Fell in Love with a Girl from San Luis.* Cenicero, Colorado.

Morgan, Nicholas C. "Mormon Colonization in the San Luis Valley," *Colorado Magazine*, Vol. 27, No. 4, October 1959, pp. 286-293

Murray, Andrew E. *A History of Presbyterianism in Colorado,* Ph.D. Thesis, Princeton Theological Seminary, 1947.

_____, *The Skyline Synod.* Denver: 1970.

National Park Service. *San Luis Valley and Central Sangre de Cristo Mountains Reconnaissance Survey Report*, Intermountain Region: 2011.

Nelson, Connie Isard. *Reverend Alexander Parley and the San Luis Valley, 1875 to 1880.* M.A. Thesis, Western State College of Colorado, Gunnison, 1982.

O'Neil, Floyd A., ed. *The Southern Utes.* Salt Lake City: 1973.

O'Ryan, Rev. William and Rev. Thomas H. Malone. *History of the Catholic Church in Colorado.* Denver: 1889.

Our Mission Field, Presbyterian Church Publication, May 1883, p. 398

Owen, Gordon R. Las Cruiuces, New Mexico 1849-1999. Privately printed by author in 1999.

_____, *Two Alberts.* Las Cruces, New Mexico: 2006.

Owens, Sister M. Lilliana. *Jesuit Beginnings in New Mexico, 1867-1882.* El Paso: 1950.

_____, ed. "The Sisters of Mercy of St. Mary's Academy, *Jesuit Studies—Southwest,* No. 2. El Paso: 1951.

Parsons, Eugene. "Progress of Education in the Colorado Territory," *The Trail* (Denver), Vol. 15, No. 10, March 1923 p. 13.

Parsons, Eugene. "Some of Colorado's Churches," *The Trail* (Denver), Vol. 15, No. 3, August 1922, p. 7.

Presbyterian Church USA, *Board of National Missions History Cards* (Spanish-speaking Southwest).

Presbyterian Home Missions, November 1879.

Presbyterian Home Missions, 1881, p. 425.

Presbyterian Home Missions, June 1882, p. 260.

Presbyterian Home Missions, October 1882, pp. 225-226

Presbyterian Home Missionary, March 1884, p. 59.

Presbyterian Home Missionary, April 1884, p. 89.

Presbyterian Home Missionary, June 1885, p. 126.

Presbyterian Home Missionary, September 1885.

Presbyterian Home Missionary, May 1886, p. 107.

Pueblo Chieftan, May 26, 1935.

_____, January 7, 1994.

Rakow, Mary Martin. *Melinda Rankin and Magadalen Hayden, Evangelical and Catholic Forms of Nineteenth Century Christian Spirituality,* Ph.D. Thesis, Boston College, 1982.

Rasch, Philip J. "Feuding at Farmington," *New Mexico Historical Review,* Vol. 40, 1965, pp. 215-229.

Record Book of Costilla County School Superintendent 1871-1892, Colorado State Archives, Denver.

Records of Session of the First Presbyterian Church of Antonito, CO, 1889-1893 (unpaged).

Rendon, Rev. Gabino. Letter to Miss Edith Agnew, dated August 24, 1953 (copy in author's possession).

Reports of the Superintendent of Public Instruction, State of Colorado, Costilla and Conejos Counties, 1878-1893, Colorado State Archives.

Revista Evangelica. Las Vegas, New Mexico, Vol. 1, No. 1, July 1877.

Revista Catolica. Las Vegas, New Mexico: November 2, 1878, p. 518.

Revista Catolica. March 26, 1879.

Revista Catolica, August 18, 1880, p. 415.

Revista Catolica, September 19, 1880, p. 435.

Rocky Mountain News (Denver), December 24, 1871.

Rocky Mountain News, February 3, 1884, pp. 2, 4.

Rocky Mountain Presbyterian, January 1878.

Rocky Mountain Presbyterian, October 1880.

Rocky Mountain Presbyterian, October 1882.

Rocky Mountain Presbyterian, September, 1885.

Ross, Anna M. Letter to Sheldon Jackson, dated May 17, 1871.

Ross, D. Reid. *Lincoln's Veteran Volunteers Win the War.* State University of New York Press, New York: 2008.

Saguache Chronicle, Vol. 3, No. 13, December 30, 1876; and Vol. 4, No. 38.

San Luis Valley Historian, Vol. X, No. 3, 1978, p. 19.

Schmitz, Richard A. "Jesuit Missionary Methods in Northwestern Mexico," *The Spanish Borderlands – A First Reader,* Oakah L. Jones Jr., ed.

Sherrill, Lewis J. *Presbyterian Parochial Schools, 1846-1870.* New York: 1969.

Simmons, Virginia M. *The San Luis Valley.* Boulder, Colorado: University Press of Colorado, 1979.

Solberg, Dustin. "Taylor Ranch Sells." *High Country News,* August 16, 1999.

Spencer, Frank C. *The Story of the San Luis Valley,* Alamosa, Colorado: San Luis Valley Historical Association, 1975.

Statuter, Msgr. Patrick C. *100 Years in Colorado's Oldest Parish.*

Stewart, Rev. Robert L. "The Mission of Sheldon Jackson," *Journal of Presbyterian History.* Vol. VI, Nos. 2 & 3. Philadelphia: June-Sept. 1911.

Stoller, Marianne L. *A Study of Nineteenth Century Hispanic Arts in the American Southwest; Appearances and Processes.* Ph.D. Thesis, University of Pennsylvania, 1979.

Swadesh, Frances L. *Hispanic Americans of the Ute Frontier from the Chama Valley to the San Juan Basin, 1694-1960,* Ph.D. Thesis, University of Colorado, 1960, p. 88.

_____, *Los Primeros Pabladores; Hispanic Americans of the Ute Frontier.* South Bend, 1974.

Sylvester, Nathaniel Bartlett. *History of Saratoga County, New York.* Interlaken, NY: 1979.

Szasz, Ferenc Morto. *The Protestant Clergy in the Great Plains and the Mountain West, 1865-1915,* Albuquerque: 1988.

Taylor, Morris P. "Campaigns against the Jicarilla Apache, 1855," *New Mexico Historical Review,* Vol. 45, No. 2, April 1970.

The Church at Home and Abroad, Vol. 11, December 1887, p.557.

The Denver Republic, Denver: December 15, 1888.

The New York Observer. New York: 1884.

The San Luis Valley (pamphlet). Salida, Colorado, 1891.

Trainer, Sister Mary Geralda. Letter dated August 3, 1953, to the *Denver Catholic Register* (copy in author's files.

Tusher, Olibama Lopez. *The People of El Valle*, El Escritorio. Denver: 1975.

US Census of Population, 1880, Costilla County.

US Statutes At Large, Vol. II, Chapter LXXV. Boston: 1863.

Valdez, Arnold and Maria Mondragon-Valdez. "Costilla County, Colorado: Contested Landscapes." http://revista.drclas.harvard.edu/book/costilla-county-colorado.

Van Diest, Edmond C. "Early History of Costilla County," *The Colorado Magazine,* Vol. 5, No. 4, August 1928.

Verdesi, Elizabeth Howell. *In But Still Out—Women In The Church.* Philadelphia: 1976.

Vigil, Charles A. *History and Folklore of San Pablo and San Pedro, Colorado,* M.A. Thesis, Adams State College, 1956.

Vigil, Ralph H. "Willa Cather and Historical Reality," *New Mexico Historical review,* Vol. 50, No. 2, 1975, pp. 125-131.

Yurtinis, John F. "Colorado, Mormons and the Mexican War," *Essays and Monographs in Colorado History,* No. 1, 1983, Colorado Historical Society, Denver.

W.Y. Brown, Colorado, January 10, 1873, SJL-4-210, Pennsylvania Historical Society.

Warnshuis, Paul L. *Along the Spanish Trail in the Southwest* New York: 1941.

Weatherby, Lela A. *A Study of the Early Years of the Presbyterian Work with the Spanish Speaking People of New Mexico and Colorado and Its Development from 1850-1920,* M.A. Thesis, Presbyterian College of Christian Education, 1942.

Welsh, E.B. *Buckeye Presbyterianism.* 1968.

Welter, Barbara. "She Hath Done What She Could," *Women in American Religion,* Janet Wilson James, ed. (Philadelphia, 1980), pp. 124, 177.

Women's Executive Committee of Home Missions, Home Mission Monthly, Vol. I, 1886-87.

_____, *Home Mission Monthly*, Vo. 2, 1887-1888.

_____, *Home Mission Monthly*, Vol. 3, 1887-89.

_____, *Home Mission Monthly,* Vol. 4, 1890-91.

_____, *Home Missions Monthly*, Vol. 5, 1892-93

_____, *Plans and Regulations,* n.d.

Yohn, Susan M. *A Contest of Faiths.* Ithaca, New York: 1995.

Zeleny, Carolyn. *Relations between the Spanish-Americans and Anglo-Americans in New Mexico (The Mexican American).* New York: Arno Press, 1984.

Author unknown. "The Wheeler Expedition in Southern Colorado," *Harpers New Monthly Magazine* (New York), Vol. 52, No. 312, May 1876.

Author unknown, "Reminiscence of Early Pueblo," *The Colorado Magazine,* Vol. 22, No. 3, May 1945.

An Historical Sketch of the Presbyteries, Churches and Mission Work of the Synod of Colorado (undated pamphlet).

Author unknown, *Historical Sketch of the Presbytery of Pueblo.* (pamphlet) Pueblo, Colorado: 1906.

INDEX

ABOUT THE AUTHOR

D. Reid Ross is a retired urban planner and family historian. The author of *Lincoln's Veteran Volunteers Win the War* (SUNY Press) and numerous articles in history journals, he has traced his family roots back to the 17th century. The story of his great-aunt Anna Marie Ross remains one of his favorites.

CPSIA information can be obtained
at www.ICGtesting.com
Printed in the USA
LVHW07s0317100918
589649LV00018B/81/P

9 780692 068496